CONTENTS

Book 1

WHY I WROTE THIS

It's surprising that this book even needs to exist. Over the course of human history, we have seen the benefits of infinite thinking so many times. The rise of great societies, advancements in science and medicine and the exploration of space all happened because large groups of people, united in common cause, chose to collaborate with no clear end in sight. If a rocket that was headed for the stars crashed, for example, we figured out what was wrong and tried again . . . and again . . . and again. And even after we succeeded, we kept going. We did these things not because of the promise of an end-of-year bonus; we did these things because we felt like we were contributing to something bigger than ourselves, something with value that would last well beyond our own lifetimes.

For all its benefits, acting with an infinite, long-term view is not easy. It takes real effort. As human beings we are naturally inclined to seek out immediate solutions to uncomfortable problems and prioritize quick wins to advance our ambitions. We tend to see the world in terms of successes and failures, winners and losers. This default win-lose mode can sometimes work for the short term; however, as a strategy for how companies and organizations operate, it can have grave consequences over the longer term.

The results of this default mindset are all too familiar: annual rounds of mass layoffs to meet arbitrary projections, cutthroat work environments, subservience to the shareholder over the needs of employees and customers, dishonest and unethical business practices, rewarding high-performing toxic team members while turning a blind eye to the damage they are doing to the rest of the team and rewarding leaders who seem to care a lot more about themselves than those in their charge. All things that contribute to a decline of loyalty and engagement and an increase of insecurity and anxiety that too many of us feel these days. This impersonal and transactional approach to business seems to have accelerated in the aftermath of the Industrial Revolution and seems to be accelerating even more in our digital age. Indeed, our entire understanding of commerce and capitalism seems to have fallen under the sway of short-term, finite-minded thinking.

Though many of us lament this state of things, unfortunately it seems like the market's desire to maintain the status quo is more powerful than the momentum to change it. When we say things like "people must come before profit," we often face resistance. Many of those who control the current system, many of our current leaders, tell us we are naïve and don't understand the "reality" of how business works. As a result, too many of us back down. We resign ourselves to waking up dreading to go to work, not feeling safe when we are there and struggling to find fulfillment in our lives. So much so that the search for that elusive work-life balance has become an entire industry unto itself. It leaves me wondering, do we have another, viable option?

It is entirely possible that perhaps, just perhaps, the "reality" the cynics keep talking about doesn't have to be that way. That perhaps our current system of doing business isn't "right," or even "best." It is just the system that we are used to, one preferred and advanced by a minority, not the majority. If this is, indeed, the case, then we have an opportunity to advance a different reality.

It is well within our power to build a world in which the vast majority of us wake up every single morning inspired, feel safe at work and return home fulfilled at the end of the day. The kind of change I advocate is not easy. But it is possible. With good leaders—great leaders—this vision can come to life. Great leaders are the ones who think beyond "short term" versus "long term." They are the ones who know that it is not about the next quarter or the next election; it is about the next generation. Great leaders set up their organizations to succeed beyond their own lifetimes, and when they do, the benefits—for us, for business and even for the shareholder—are extraordinary.

I wrote this book not to convert those who defend the status quo, I wrote this book to rally those who are ready to challenge that status quo and replace it with a reality that is vastly more conducive to our deep-seated human need to feel safe, to contribute to something bigger than ourselves and to provide for ourselves and our families. A reality that works for our best interests as individuals, as companies, as communities and as a species.

If we believe in a world in which we can feel inspired, safe and fulfilled every single day and if we believe that leaders are the ones who can deliver on that vision, then it is our collective responsibility to find, guide and support those who are committed to leading in a way that will more likely bring that vision to life. And one of the steps we need to take is to learn what it means to lead in the Infinite Game.

Simon Sinek
February 4, 2019
London, England

WINNING

On the morning of January 30, 1968, North Vietnam launched a surprise attack against U.S. and allied forces. Over the next twenty-four hours, more than 85,000 North Vietnamese and Viet Cong troops attacked over 125 targets across the country. The American forces were caught completely off guard. So much so that many of the commanding officers weren't even at their posts when the attacks began—they were away celebrating Tét in nearby cities. The Tét Offensive had begun.

Tét is the Lunar New Year and it is as significant to the Vietnamese as Christmas is to many Westerners. And, like the Christmas truce of World War I, there was a decades-old tradition in Vietnam that there was never any fighting on Tét. However, seeing an opportunity to overwhelm American forces and hopefully bring a swift end to the war, North Vietnamese leadership decided to break with tradition when they launched their surprise offensive.

Here's the amazing thing: the United States repelled every single attack. Every single one. And American troops didn't just repel the onslaughts, they decimated the attacking forces. After most of the major fighting had come to an end, about a week after the initial attack, America had lost fewer than a thousand troops. North Vietnam, in stark contrast, lost over 35,000 troops! In the city of Hué, where fighting continued for almost a month, America lost 150 Marines compared to an estimated 5,000 troops the North Vietnamese lost!

A close examination of the Vietnam War as a whole reveals a remarkable picture. America actually won the vast majority of the battles it fought. Over the course of the ten years in which U.S. troops were active in the Vietnam War, America lost 58,000 troops. North Vietnam lost over 3 million people. As a percent of population, that's the equivalent of America losing 27 million people in 1968.

All this begs the question, how do you win almost
every battle, decimate your enemy and still lose the war?

All this begs the question, how do you win almost
every battle, decimate your enemy and still lose the war?

Chapter 1

FINITE AND INFINITE GAMES

f there are at least two players, a game exists. And there are two kinds of games: finite games and infinite games.

Finite games are played by known players. They have fixed rules. And there is an agreed-upon objective that, when reached, ends the game. Football, for example, is a finite game. The players all wear uniforms and are easily identifiable. There is a set of rules, and referees are there to enforce those rules. All the players have agreed to play by those rules and they accept penalties when they break the rules. Everyone agrees that whichever team has scored more points by the end of the set time period will be declared the winner, the game will end and everyone will go home. In finite games, there is always a beginning, a middle and an end.

Infinite games, in contrast, are played by known and unknown players. There are no exact or agreed-upon rules. Though there may be conventions or laws that govern how the players conduct themselves, within those broad boundaries, the players can operate however they want. And if they choose to break with convention, they can. The manner in which each player chooses to play is entirely up to them. And they can change how they play the game at any time, for any reason.

Infinite games have infinite time horizons. And because there is no finish line, no practical end to the game, there is no such thing as "winning" an infinite game. In an infinite game, the primary objective is to keep playing, to perpetuate the game.

My understanding of these two types of games comes from the master himself, Professor James P. Carse, who penned a little treatise called *Finite and Infinite Games: A Vision of Life as Play and Possibility* in 1986. It was Carse's book that first got me thinking beyond winning and losing, beyond ties and stalemates. The more I looked at our world through Carse's lens of finite and infinite games, the more I started to see infinite games all around us, games with no finish lines and no winners. There is no such thing as coming in first in marriage or friendship, for example. Though school may be finite, there is no such thing as winning education. We can beat out other candidates for a job or promotion, but no one is ever crowned the winner of careers. Though nations may compete on a global scale with other nations for land, influence or economic advantage, there is no such thing as winning global politics. No matter how successful we are in life, when we die, none of us will be declared the winner of life. And there is certainly no such thing as winning business. All these things are journeys, not events.

However, if we listen to the language of so many of our leaders today, it's as if they don't know the game in which they are playing. They talk constantly about "winning." They obsess about "beating their competition." They announce to the world that they are "the best." They state that their vision is to "be number one." Except that in games without finish lines, all of these things are impossible.

When we lead with a finite mindset in an infinite game, it leads to all kinds of problems, the most common of which include the decline of trust, cooperation and innovation. Leading with an infinite mindset in an infinite game, in contrast, really does move us in a better direction. Groups that adopt an infinite mindset enjoy vastly higher levels of trust, cooperation and innovation and all the subsequent benefits. If we are all, at various times, players in infinite games, then it is in our interest to learn how to recognize the game we are in and what it takes to lead with an infinite mindset. It is equally important for us to learn to recognize the clues when finite thinking exists so that we can make adjustments before real damage is done.

The Infinite Game of Business

The game of business fits the very definition of an infinite game. We may not know all of the other players and new ones can join the game at any time. All the players determine their own strategies and tactics and there is no set of fixed rules to which everyone has agreed, other than the law (and even that can vary from country to country). Unlike a finite game, there is no predetermined beginning, middle or end to business. Although many of us agree to certain time frames for evaluating our own performance relative to that of other players—the financial year, for example—those time frames represent markers within the course of the game; none marks the end of the game itself. The game of business has no finish line.

Despite the fact that companies are playing in a game that cannot be won, too many business leaders keep playing as if they can. They continue to make claims that they are the "best" or that they are "number one." Such claims have become so commonplace that we rarely, if ever, stop to actually think about how ridiculous some of them are. Whenever I see a company claim that it is number one or the best, I always like to look at the fine print to see how they cherry-picked the metrics. For years, British Airways, for example, claimed in their advertising that they were "the world's favourite airline." Richard Branson's airline, Virgin Atlantic, filed a dispute with Britain's Advertising Standards Authority that such a claim could not be true based on recent passenger surveys. The ASA allowed the claim to stand, however, on the basis that British Airways carried more international passengers than any other airline. "Favourite," as they used the word, meant that their operation was expansive, not necessarily preferred.

To one company, being number one may be based on the number of customers they serve. To another, it could be about revenues, stock performance, the number of employees or the number of offices they have around the globe. The companies making the claims even get to decide the time frames in which they are making their calculations. Sometimes it's a quarter. Or eight months. Sometimes a year. Or five years. Or a dozen. But did everyone else in their industry agree to those same time frames for comparison? In finite games, there's a single, agreed-upon metric that separates the winner from the loser, things like goals scored, speed or strength. In infinite games, there are multiple metrics, which is why we can never declare a winner.

In a finite game, the game ends when its time is up and the players live on to play another day (unless it was a duel, of course). In an infinite game, it's the opposite. It is the game that lives on and it is the players whose time runs out. Because there is no such thing as winning or losing in an infinite game, the players simply drop out of the game when they run out of the will and resources to keep playing. In business we call this bankruptcy or sometimes merger or acquisition. Which means, to succeed in the Infinite Game of business, we have to stop thinking about who wins or who's the best and start thinking about how to build organizations that are strong enough and healthy enough to stay in the game for many generations to come. The benefits of which, ironically, often make companies stronger in the near term also.

A Tale of Two Players

Some years ago, I spoke at an education summit for Microsoft. A few months later, I spoke at an education summit for Apple. At the Microsoft event, the majority of the presenters devoted a good portion of their presentations to talking about how they were going to beat Apple. At the Apple event, 100 percent of the presenters spent 100 percent of their time talking about how Apple was trying to help teachers teach and help students learn. One group seemed obsessed with beating their competition. The other group seemed obsessed with advancing a cause.

After my talk at Microsoft, they gave me a gift—the new Zune (when it was still a thing). This was Microsoft's answer to Apple's iPod, the dominant player in the MP3-player market at the time. Not to be outdone, Microsoft introduced the Zune to try to steal market share from their archrival. Though he knew it wouldn't be easy, in 2006, then CEO of Microsoft Steve Ballmer was confident that Microsoft could eventually "beat" Apple. And if the quality of the product was the only factor, Ballmer was right to be optimistic. The version Microsoft gave me—the Zune HD—was, I have to admit, quite exceptional. It was elegantly designed. The user interface was simple, intuitive and user-friendly. I really, really liked it. (In the interest of full disclosure, I gave it away to a friend for the simple reason that unlike my iPod, which was compatible with Microsoft Windows, the Zune was not compatible with iTunes. So as much as I wanted to use it, I couldn't.)

After my talk at the Apple event, I shared a taxi back to the hotel with a senior Apple executive, employee number 54 to be exact, meaning he'd been at the company since the early days and was completely immersed in Apple's culture and belief set. Sitting there with him, a captive audience, I couldn't help myself. I had to stir the pot a little. So I turned to him and said, "You know . . . I spoke at Microsoft and they gave me their new Zune, and I have to tell you, it is *SO MUCH BETTER* than your iPod touch." The executive looked at me, smiled, and replied, "I have no doubt." And that was it. The conversation was over.

The Apple exec was unfazed by the fact that Microsoft had a better product. Perhaps he was just displaying the arrogance of a dominant market leader. Perhaps he was putting on an act (a very good one). Or perhaps there was something else at play. Although I didn't know it at the time, his response was consistent with that of a leader with an infinite mindset.

The Benefits of an Infinite Mindset

In the Infinite Game, the true value of an organization cannot be measured by the success it has achieved based on a set of arbitrary metrics over arbitrary time frames. The true value of an organization is measured by the desire others have to contribute to that organization's ability to keep succeeding, not just during the time they are there, but well beyond their own tenure. While a finite-minded leader works to get something from their employees, customers and shareholders in order to meet arbitrary metrics, the infinite-minded leader works to ensure that their employees, customers and shareholders remain inspired to continue contributing with their effort, their wallets and their investments. Players with an infinite mindset want to leave their organizations in better shape than they found them. Lego invented a toy that has stood the test of time not because it was lucky, but because nearly everyone who works there wants to do things to ensure that the company will survive them. Their drive is not to beat the quarter, their drive is to "continue to create innovative play experiences and reach more children every year."

According to Carse, a finite-minded leader plays to end the game—to win. And if they want to be the winner, then there has to be a loser. They play for themselves and want to defeat the other players. They make every plan and every move with winning in mind. They almost always believe they *must* act that way, even though, in fact, they don't have to at all. There is no rule that says they have to act that way. It is their mindset that directs them.

Carse's infinite player plays to keep playing. In business, that means building an organization that can survive its leaders. Carse also expects the infinite player to play for the good of the game. In business, that means seeing beyond the bottom line. Where a finite-minded player makes products they think they can sell to people, the infinite-minded player makes products that people want to buy. The former is primarily focused on how the sale of those products benefits the company; the latter is primarily focused on how the products benefit those who buy them.

Finite-minded players tend to follow standards that help them achieve their personal goals with less regard to the effects of the ripples that may cause. To ask, "What's best for me" is finite thinking. To ask, "What's best for us" is infinite thinking. A company built for the Infinite Game doesn't think of itself alone. It considers the impact of its decisions on its people, its community, the economy, the country and the world. It does these things for the good of the game. George Eastman, the founder of Kodak, was devoted to his vision of making photography easy and accessible to everyone. He also recognized that advancing his vision was intimately tied to the well-being of his people and the community in which they lived. In 1912, Kodak was the first company to pay employees a dividend based on company performance and several years later issued what we now know as stock options. They also provided their employees with a generous benefits package, gave paid time off for sick leave (it was a new idea then) and subsidized tuitions for employees who took classes at local colleges. (All things that have been adopted by many other companies. In other words, it was not only good for Kodak, it was good for the game of business.) In addition to the tens of thousands of jobs Kodak provided, Eastman built a hospital, founded a music school, and gave generously to institutions of higher learning, including the Mechanics Institute of Rochester (which was later renamed Rochester Institute of Technology) and the University of Rochester.

Because they are playing with an end point in mind, Carse tells us, finite-minded players do not like surprises and fear any kind of disruption. Things they cannot predict or cannot control could upset their plans and increase their chances of losing. The infinite-minded player, in contrast, expects surprises, even revels in them, and is prepared to be transformed by them. They embrace the freedom of play and are open to any possibility that keeps them in the game. Instead of looking for ways to react to what has already happened, they look for ways to do something new. An infinite perspective frees us from fixating on what other companies are doing, which allows us to focus on a larger vision. Instead of reacting to how new technology will challenge our business model, for example, those with infinite mindsets are better able to foresee the applications of new technology.

It's easy now to see why the Apple executive with whom I shared a cab could be so nonchalant about Microsoft's well-designed Zune. He understood that, in the Infinite Game of business, sometimes Apple would have the better product, sometimes another company would have the better product. They weren't trying to outdo Microsoft; Apple was trying to outdo itself. The company was looking ahead to what would come after the iPod. Apple's infinite mindset helped them think, not outside the box, but beyond it. About a year after the Zune was first introduced, Apple released the first iPhone. The iPhone redefined the entire category of smartphones and rendered both the Zune and the iPod virtually obsolete. Though some people believed Apple could predict consumer preferences and see into the future, they couldn't. In reality it was their infinite perspective that opened a path for them to innovate in ways that companies with more finite-minded leadership simply could not.

A finite-focused company may come up with "innovative" ways to boost the bottom line, but those decisions don't usually benefit the organization, the employees, the customers and the community—those who exist beyond the bottom line. Nor do they necessarily leave the organization in better shape for the future. And the reason is simple. It's because those decisions tend to be made primarily for the benefit of the people who made them and not with the infinite future in mind . . . just the near future. In contrast, infinite-minded leaders don't ask their people to fixate on finite goals; they ask their people to help them figure out a way to advance toward a more infinite vision of the future that benefits everyone. The finite goals become the markers of progress toward that vision. And when everyone focuses on the infinite vision, it not only drives innovation, but it also drives up the numbers. Indeed, companies led by infinite-minded leaders often enjoy record-making profits. What's more, the inspiration, innovation, cooperation, brand loyalty and profits that result from infinite-minded leadership serve companies not just in times of stability but also in times of instability. The same things that help the company survive and thrive during good times help make the company strong and resilient in hard times.

A company built for resilience is a company that is structured to last forever. This is different from a company built for stability. Stability, by its very definition, is about remaining the same. A stable organization can theoretically weather a storm, then come out of it the same as it was before. In more practical terms, when a company is described as stable, it is usually to draw a contrast to another company that is higher risk and higher performing. "Slow growth but stable," so goes the thinking. But a company built for stability still fails to understand the nature of the Infinite Game, for it is likely still not prepared for the unpredictable—for the new technology, new competitor, market shift or world events that can, in an instant, derail their strategy. An infinite-minded leader does not simply want to build a company that can weather change but one that can be transformed by it. They want to build a company that embraces surprises and adapts with them. Resilient companies may come out the other end of upheaval entirely different than they were when they went in (and are often grateful for the transformation).

Victorinox, the Swiss company that made the Swiss Army knife famous, saw its business dramatically affected by the events of September 11. The ubiquitous corporate promotional item and standard gift for retirements, birthdays and graduations, in an instant, was banned from our hand luggage. Whereas most companies would take a defensive posture—fixating on the blow to their traditional model and how much it was going to cost them —Victorinox took the offense. They embraced the surprise as an opportunity rather than a threat—a characteristic move of an infinite-minded player. Rather than employing extreme cost cutting and laying off their workforce, the leaders of Victorinox came up with innovative ways to save jobs (they made no layoffs at all), increased investment in new product development and inspired their people to imagine how they could leverage their brand into new markets.

In good times, Victorinox built up reserves of cash, knowing that at some point there would be more difficult times. As CEO Carl Elsener says, "When you look at the history of world economics, it was always like this. Always! And in the future, it will always be like this. It will never go only up. It will never go only down. It will go up and down and up and down. . . . We do not think in quarters," he says. "We think in generations." This kind of infinite thinking put Victorinox in a position where they were both philosophically and financially ready to face what for another company might have been a fatal crisis. And the result was astonishing. Victorinox is now a different and even stronger company than it was before September 11. Knives used to account for 95 percent of the company's total sales (Swiss Army knives alone accounted for 80 percent). Today, Swiss Army knives account for only 35 percent of total revenue, but sales of travel gear, watches and fragrances have helped Victorinox nearly double its revenues compared to the days before September 11. Victorinox is not a stable company, it is a resilient one.

The benefits of playing with an infinite mindset are clear and multifaceted. So what happens when we play with a finite mindset in the Infinite Game of business?

The Detriments of a Finite Mindset in an Infinite Game

Decades after the Vietnam War, Robert McNamara, U.S. Secretary of Defense during the war, had the chance to meet Nguyen Co Thach, the North Vietnamese Foreign Ministry's chief specialist on the United States from 1960 to 1975. McNamara was flabbergasted by how badly America misunderstood their enemy. "You must never have read a history book," McNamara recounts Thach scolding him. "If you had, you'd know we weren't pawns of the Chinese or the Russians. . . . Don't you understand that we have been fighting the Chinese for a thousand years?" Thach went on. "We were fighting for our independence! And we would fight to the last man! And we were determined to do so! And no amount of bombing, no amount of U.S. pressure would ever have stopped us!" The North Vietnamese were playing an infinite game with an infinite mindset.

The United States assumed the Vietnam War was finite because most wars are, indeed, finite. In most wars there is a land grab or some other easy to measure finite objective. If the combatants enter the war with clear political objectives, whoever achieves their finite objective first will be declared victor, a treaty will be signed and the war will end. But that's not always the case. Had America's leaders paid closer attention, perhaps they would have recognized the true nature of the Vietnam War sooner. There were clues all around.

For starters, there was no clear beginning, middle and end to America's involvement in Vietnam. Nor was there a clear political objective that, when achieved, would allow them to declare victory and bring their troops home. And even if there had been, the North Vietnamese would not have agreed to it. The Americans also seem to have misunderstood who they were fighting against. They believed the conflict in Vietnam was a proxy war against China and the Soviet Union. But the North Vietnamese were ardent that they were no puppet of any other government. Vietnam had been fighting against imperialist influence for decades, against the Japanese during World War II, then against the French afterward. To the North Vietnamese, the war with the United States wasn't an extension of the Cold War; it was a fight against yet another interventionist power. Even the manner in which the North Vietnamese fought—their propensity to disobey the conventions of traditional warfare and their will to keep fighting no matter how many people they lost—should have signaled to America's leaders that they had misjudged the nature of the game they were in.

When we play with a finite mindset in an infinite game, the odds increase that we will find ourselves in a quagmire, racing through the will and resources we need to keep playing. And this is what happened to America in Vietnam. The United States operated as if the game were finite instead of fighting against a player that was playing with the right mindset for the Infinite Game they were actually in. While America was fighting to "win," the North Vietnamese were fighting for their lives! And both made strategic choices according to their mindset. Despite their vastly superior military might, there was simply no way the United States could prevail. What brought America's involvement in Vietnam to an end was not a military or political win or loss, but public pressure back home. The American people could no longer support a seemingly unwinnable and expensive war in a faraway land. It's not that America "lost" the Vietnam War, rather it had exhausted the will and resources to keep playing . . . and so it was forced to drop out of the game.

The Quagmire of Vietnam in Business

When Microsoft launched the Zune, there was no grand vision that the product was helping to advance. They weren't thinking about what possibilities the future might hold. It was just a competition for market share and money—one in which Microsoft wasn't doing very well. Ballmer's prediction that the Zune could "beat" the iPod couldn't have been more wrong. Debuting with a 9 percent market share, the Zune's popularity declined steadily until it hit 1 percent in 2010. The following year it was discontinued. The iPod, in contrast, enjoyed around a 70 percent slice for the same time period.

Some have argued that the Zune failed because Microsoft didn't invest enough in advertising. But the theory doesn't hold up. Spanx, Sriracha, and GoPro are just three brands that relied solely on word of mouth to increase brand awareness. All three not only emerged from obscurity without traditional advertising, but went on to thrive without it. Others suggest that the Zune failed because Microsoft was too late to the MP3 player market. This theory doesn't hold up much better. Apple itself introduced the iPod a full five years after MP3 players were a well-known product category. Brands like Rio, Nomad and Sony were already advancing the technology and selling well. Yet, within four years of its 2001 launch, the iPod had gained the lion's share of the U.S. digital music player market . . . a number that only continued to rise.

As great as Microsoft's Zune may have been, it wasn't the design, marketing or the timing of the product that were the problem. It takes more than all those things to survive and thrive in the Infinite Game of business. Great products fail all the time. How a company is led must also be considered. Prioritizing comparison and winning above all else, finite-minded leaders will set corporate strategy, product strategy, incentive structures and hiring decisions to help meet finite goals. And with a finite mindset firmly entrenched in almost all aspects of the organization, a sort of tunnel vision results. The result of which pushes almost everyone inside the company to place excessive focus on the urgent at the expense of the important. Executives instinctively start to respond to known factors instead of exploring or advancing unknown possibilities. And in some cases, leaders can become so obsessed with what the competition is doing, falsely believing they need to react to their every move, that they become blind to a whole host of better choices to strengthen their own organization. It's like trying to win by playing defense. Seduced by a finite mindset, Microsoft found themselves in a never-ending game of whack-a-mole.

Microsoft's leaders failed to appreciate the Infinite Game they were in and the infinite mindset with which Apple was playing. Though Steve Ballmer sometimes spoke of "vision" or the "long term," like other finite-minded leaders who use this kind of infinite language, he almost always did so in the finite context of rank, stock performance, market share and money. Playing with the wrong mindset for the game they were in, Microsoft was chasing an impossible objective—"to win." Wasting the will and resources needed to stay in the game, like America in Vietnam, Microsoft was in quagmire.

It seemed the company had not learned its lesson with the iPod. When the iPhone came out in 2007, Ballmer's reaction to it underscored his finite perspective. Questioned about the iPhone in an interview, he scoffed, "There's no chance that the iPhone is going to get any significant market share. No chance. . . . They may make a lot of money. But if you actually take a look at the 1.3 billion phones that get sold, I'd prefer to have our software in 60% or 70% or 80% of them, than I would to have 2% or 3%, which is what Apple might get." Constrained by a finite mindset, Ballmer was more focused on the relative numbers the iPhone could achieve instead of seeing how it might alter the entire market . . . or even completely redefine the role our phones play in our lives. In a turn of events that must have driven Ballmer crazy, after just five years on the market, iPhone sales alone were higher than all of Microsoft's products combined.

In 2013, at his final press conference as CEO of Microsoft, Steve Ballmer summed up his career in a most finite-minded way. He defined success based on the metrics he selected within the time frame of his own tenure in the job. "In the last five years, probably Apple has made more money than we have," he said. "But in the last thirteen years, I bet we've made more money than almost anybody on the planet. And that, frankly, is a great source of pride to me." It seems Ballmer was trying to say that under the thirteen years of his leadership, his company had "won." Imagine how different that press conference could have been if, instead of looking back at a balance sheet, Ballmer shared all the things Microsoft had done and could still do to advance Bill Gates's original infinite vision: "To empower every person and every organization on the planet to achieve more."

A finite-minded leader uses the company's performance to demonstrate the value of their own career. An infinite-minded leader uses their career to enhance the long-term value of the company . . . and only part of that value is counted in money. The game didn't end simply because Ballmer retired. The company continued to play without him. In the Infinite Game, how well he did financially is much less important than whether he left the company culture adequately prepared to survive and thrive for the next thirteen years. Or thirty-three years. Or three hundred years. And on that standard, Ballmer lost.

In the Infinite Game of business, when our leaders maintain a finite mindset or put too much focus on finite objectives, they may be able to achieve a number one ranking with an arbitrary metric over an arbitrary time frame. But that doesn't necessarily mean they are doing the things they need to ensure that the company can keep playing for as long as possible. In fact, more often than not, the things they do harm the company's inner workings and, without intervention, accelerate the company's ultimate demise.

Because finite-minded leaders place unbalanced focus on near-term results, they often employ any strategy or tactic that will help them make the numbers. Some favorite options include reducing investment in research and development, extreme cost cutting (e.g., regular rounds of layoffs, opting for cheaper, lower quality ingredients in products, cutting corners in manufacturing or quality control), growth through acquisition and stock buybacks. These decisions can, in turn, shake a company's culture. People start to realize that nothing and no one is safe. In response, some instinctually behave as if they were switched to self-preservation mode. They may hoard information, hide mistakes and operate in a more cautious, risk-averse way. To protect themselves, they trust no one. Others double down on an only-the-fittest-survive mentality. Their tactics can become overly aggressive. Their egos become unchecked. They learn to manage up the hierarchy to garner favor with senior leadership while, in some cases, sabotaging their own colleagues. To protect themselves, they trust no one. Regardless of whether they are in self-preservation or self-promotion mode, the sum of all of these behaviors contributes to a general decline in cooperation across the company, which also leads to stagnation of any truly new or innovative ideas. This is what happened at Microsoft.

Consumed by the finite game, Microsoft became obsessed with quarterly numbers. Many of the people who had been at the company from the early days lamented a loss of inspiration, imagination and innovation. Trust and cooperation suffered as internal product groups started to fight with each other instead of supporting each other. And as if large companies don't struggle enough with silos, Microsoft's divisions sometimes actively worked to undermine each other. It went from being a place that attracted people to join a crusade to a place that the best and brightest avoided like the plague. A company that used to be a "lean competition machine led by young visionaries of unparalleled talent," as *Vanity Fair* reported, "mutated into something bloated and bureaucracy-laden, with an internal culture that unintentionally rewards managers who strangle innovative ideas that might threaten the established order of things." In other words, a finite mindset left the company culture a mess.

It can take a long time for very large companies with a finite-minded leader at the helm to exhaust the will and resources accumulated by the infinite leader that preceded them. Under Ballmer, Microsoft was still a dominant player, especially in business markets. This was largely thanks to the groundwork laid under the more infinite-minded Bill Gates. Had Ballmer stayed, or another finite leader replaced him, however, the will of the people to keep fighting the good fight and the resources the company would need to keep playing would eventually have run out. Just because a company is big and has enjoyed financial success does not mean it is strong enough to last.

Microsoft's experience is not unique. Business history is littered with similar cautionary tales. General Motors' obsession with market share over profit, for example, would have put them out of business if it weren't for a government bailout. Sears, Circuit City, Lehman Brothers, Eastern Airlines and Blockbuster Video were not so lucky. They are just a few more examples of once strong, well-established companies whose leaders were seduced by the thrill of playing with a finite mindset only to put their companies on a path to destruction.

Sadly, over the course of the past thirty to forty years, finite-minded leadership has become the modern standard in business. Finite-minded leadership is embraced by Wall Street and taught in business schools. At the same time, the life span of companies appears to be getting shorter and shorter. According to a study by McKinsey, the average life span of an S&P 500 company has dropped over forty years since the 1950s, from an average of sixty-one years to less than eighteen years today. And according to Professor Richard Foster of Yale University, the rate of change "is at a faster pace than ever." I accept there are multiple factors that contribute to these numbers, but we must consider that too many leaders today are building companies that are simply not made to last. Which is ironic because even the most goal-oriented, finite-minded leader must concede that the longer an organization can survive and thrive, the more likely it is to achieve *all* its goals.

It's not just companies that are impacted by too much finite-minded leadership. With more finite thinkers in positions of authority in all facets of life comes increased pressure to change public policy to further entrench even more finite-mindedness.

And before too long, we have an entire economy operating within the constraints of a finite mindset, playing by the rules for a game we are not in. This is an untenable situation. And the data reflects it. After the 1929 stock market crash that lead to the Great Depression, for example, the Glass-Steagall Act was introduced to curb some of the more finite-minded corporate behaviors that were the cause of the instability in the markets at that time. Between the time Glass-Steagall was passed until the 1980s and '90s, when the act was virtually gutted in the name of opening up the financial markets, the number of stock market crashes that happened was zero. Since the gutting, however, we have had three: Black Monday in 1987, the burst of the dot-com bubble in 2000 and the financial crisis of 2008.

When we play with a finite mindset in the Infinite Game, we will continue to make decisions that sabotage our own ambitions. It's like eating too many desserts in the name of "enjoying life" only to make oneself diabetic in the process. Creating the conditions for a stock market crash are an extreme example of what happens when too many players in the game opt to play with a finite mindset. The more likely scenario is a general decline in trust, cooperation and innovation in an organization, all of which make it vastly more difficult to survive and thrive in a fast-moving business world. If we believe trust, cooperation and innovation matter to the long-term prospects of our organizations, then we have only one choice—to learn how to play with an infinite mindset.

Lead with an Infinite Mindset

There are three factors we must always consider when deciding how we want to lead:

1. We don't get to choose whether a particular game is finite or infinite.

2. We do get to choose whether or not we want join the game.

3. Should we choose to join the game, we can choose whether we want to play with a finite or an infinite mindset.

If we join a finite game, clearly we want to play by the right rules in order to increase our chances of winning. There is no use preparing to play basketball if we are about to enter a game of football. The same is true if we decide to become a leader in an infinite game. We are more likely to survive and thrive if we play for the game we are in.

The choice to lead with an infinite mindset is less like preparing for a football game and more like the decision to get into shape. There is no one thing we can do in order to get into shape. We can't simply go to the gym for nine hours and expect to be in shape. However, if we go to the gym every single day for twenty minutes, we will absolutely get into shape. Consistency becomes more important than intensity. The problem is, no one knows exactly when we will see results. In fact, different people will show results at different times. But without question, 100 percent, we all know it will work. And though we may have finite fitness goals we want to reach, if we want to be as healthy as possible, the lifestyle we adopt matters more than whether or not we hit our goal on the arbitrary dates we set. With any health regime, there are certain things we have to do—eat more vegetables, work out on a regular basis and get enough sleep, for example. Adopting an infinite mindset is exactly the same.

Any leader who wants to adopt an infinite mindset must follow five essential practices:

- Advance a Just Cause
- Build Trusting Teams
- Study your Worthy Rivals
- Prepare for Existential Flexibility
- Demonstrate the Courage to Lead

If we want to follow a health regime, we can choose to follow some of the practices but not all of them—we can exercise but never eat vegetables, for example. If we choose this approach, we may get some benefit. But we will only enjoy the full benefit if we do everything. Likewise, there is a benefit to following some of the practices required for infinite thinking. However, to fully equip an organization for a long and healthy life in the Infinite Game, we must do it all.

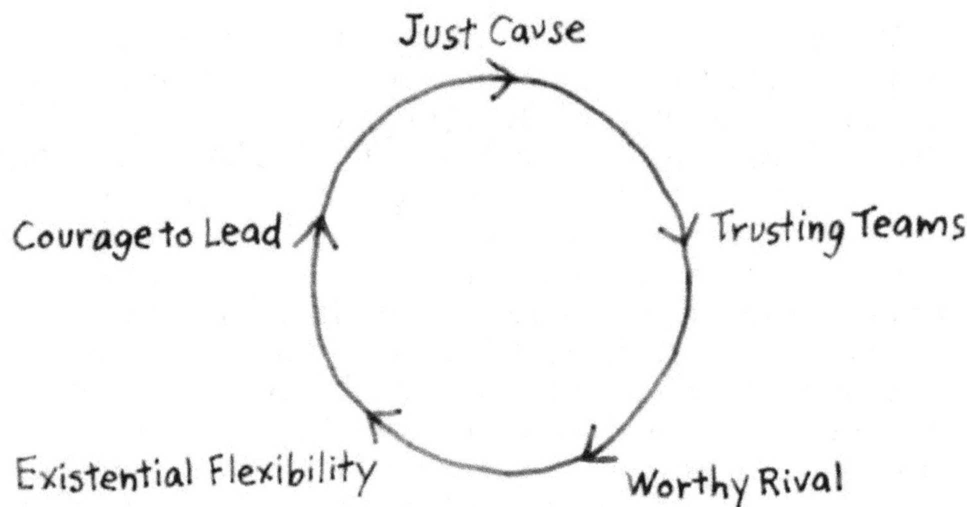

Maintaining an infinite mindset is hard. Very hard. It is to be expected that we will stray from the path. We are human and we are fallible. We are subject to bouts of greed, fear, ambition, ignorance, external pressure, competing interests, ego . . . the list goes on. To complicate matters further, finite games are seductive; they can be fun and exciting and sometimes even addictive. Just like gambling, every win, every goal hit releases a shot of dopamine in our bodies, encouraging us to play the same way again. To try to win again. We must be strong to resist that urge.

We cannot expect that we or *every* leader will lead with a perfectly infinite mindset, or that *any* leader with an infinite mindset will be able to maintain that mindset at all times. Just as it is easier to focus on a fixed, finite goal than an infinite vision of the future, it is easier to lead a company with a finite mindset, especially during times of struggle or downturn. Indeed, every one of the examples I cite in this chapter, including the affirmative examples, has, at some point in their history, been led by someone who abandoned the infinite foundation upon which the company was built to focus on more finite pursuits. In fact, finite-mindedness nearly destroyed all of these companies. Only the lucky ones that were rescued by an infinite-minded leader have gone on to become even stronger versions of themselves, more inspiring for the people who work there and more appealing to the people who buy their products.

Regardless of how we choose to play, it is essential that we be honest with ourselves and others about our choice—for our choice makes ripples. Only when those around us—our colleagues, customers and investors—know how we have chosen to play can they adjust their expectations and behaviors accordingly. Only when they know the mindset we have adopted can they figure out the short- and long-term implications for themselves. They are entitled to know how we will play so that they may make smarter decisions about who they want to work for, buy from or invest in. When they see that we have embraced the five practices of an infinite-minded leader, they can be confident that we are focused on where we are going and committed to taking care of each other along the way. They can also be confident that we will strive to resist short-term temptations and act ethically as we build our organizations to survive and thrive for a very, very long time to come.

As for us, those who choose to embrace an infinite mindset, our journey is one that will lead us to feel inspired every morning, safe when we are at work and fulfilled at the end of each day. And when it is our time to leave the game, we will look back at our lives and our careers and say, "I lived a life worth living." And more important, when imagining what the future holds, we will see how many people we've inspired to carry on the journey without us.

Chapter 2

JUST CAUSE

First they ate the animals in the zoo. Then they ate their cats and dogs. Some even resorted to eating wallpaper paste and boiled leather. Then the unthinkable. "A child died, he was just three years old," wrote Daniil Granin, one of the survivors. "His mother laid the body inside the double-glazed window and sliced off a piece of him every day to feed her second child."

These were some of the extremes the people of Leningrad were driven to during the Nazis' nearly nine-hundred-day siege of the city from September 1941 to January 1944. Over a million citizens, including four hundred thousand children, died, many of them due to starvation. And all the while, unbeknownst to the masses, a stash of hundreds of thousands of seeds and tons of potatoes, rice, nuts and cereal lay hidden in the heart of the city.

About twenty-five years before the siege began, a young botanist named Nikolai Vavilov started building his seed collection. Growing up in a time when Russia was ravaged by major famines that killed millions of people, he committed his life and his work to ending hunger and preventing future ecological disasters. What started as idealism eventually became a highly focused cause for Vavilov. He traveled the world to collect various types of food crops and learn more about what made some more resilient than others. Before long he had collected seeds from over six thousand types of crops. He also started to study genetics and experimented with developing new strains of crops that could better resist pests or disease, grow more quickly, withstand harsh conditions or offer higher yields of food. As his work advanced, Vavilov's vision for a seed bank crystallized. Just as we keep a backup of important data should our computer crash, Vavilov wanted to have a backup of the seeds for all the world's food should any species become extinct or ungrowable due to natural or man-made disasters.

Having built up quite a reputation (and an even larger seed collection), in 1920 Vavilov left his life as an academic to become the head of the Department of Applied Botany in Leningrad. With the help of government funding, Vavilov was able to bring together a whole team of scientists to join him in his work and help advance his cause. Upon his arrival at the institution, Vavilov wrote, "I would like the Department to be a necessary institution, as useful to everybody as possible. I'd like to gather the varietal diversity from all over the world, [organize them all and] turn the Department into the treasury of all crops and other floras." And like any good visionary with an infinite mindset, he concluded, "The outcome is uncertain. . . . But still, I want to try."

Within two years, however, things had changed. This was Joseph Stalin's Soviet Union, and no one was safe. Not even the highly respected Vavilov. Over the course of his rule, which lasted from 1922 until his death in 1953, Stalin is said to have been responsible for the deaths of over 20 million of his own people. And sadly, the scientist who had devoted his life to helping his country's people found himself one of Stalin's political targets. Arrested in 1940 on trumped-up charges of espionage, Vavilov was subjected to over four hundred sessions of brutal interrogation, some lasting thirteen hours, all with the intent to break his spirit and coerce a confession that he was an anti-Stalin sympathizer. But Vavilov was not a man who could be easily broken, not even under such extreme conditions. Despite his captors' best efforts, Vavilov never broke. He never confessed to the false charges against him. Sadly, in 1943, at only fifty-five years old, the visionary botanist and plant geneticist who had devoted his life to ending hunger died in prison of malnutrition.

At the time of Vavilov's death, the siege of Leningrad was raging. There, in the middle of a war zone, hidden in a rather nondescript building in St. Isaac's Square, were the records of all the work Vavilov's team had done, and of course, their priceless seed collection, which now consisted of hundreds of thousands of varieties of crops. Beyond the obvious risks from shelling, the collection was also threatened by an explosion of rats in the city (the starving people had eaten all the cats, which would ordinarily control the rat population). And as if that weren't enough, Vavilov's collection had also caught the attention of the Nazis. Obsessed with eugenics and his own health, Hitler knew the value of the seed bank and wanted it for himself and for Germany. The problem was, although Hitler knew of its existence, he did not know its location. So he tasked a group within his army to find it.

Despite the threats, and despite being subjected to the same grueling conditions as all the other residents of Leningrad, Vavilov's team of scientists continued their work throughout the siege. They ventured out in the middle of winter, for instance, to resow secret plots of potatoes in a field near the front lines. Though they were able to smuggle some of their work out of the city, the rest they kept hidden and under guard. The scientists were so devoted to Vavilov's vision that they were prepared to protect the seed bank at any cost. Even if the cost was their lives. In the end, surrounded by hundreds of thousands of seeds, tons of potatoes, rice, nuts, cereals and other crops that they refused to eat, nine of the scientists died of starvation.

When talking about his cause, Vavilov was once quoted as saying, "We shall go into the pyre, we shall burn, but we shall not retreat from our convictions." And those who joined him in common cause were more than inspired by Vavilov's words. They lived them. One of the survivors, Vadim Lekhnovich, who helped plant the seed potatoes and stood guard over them while shots flew through the air, was later asked about not eating the bounty. "It was hard to walk. It was unbearably hard to get up every morning, to move your hands and feet," he said, "but it was not in the least difficult to refrain from eating up the collection. For it was *impossible* [to think of] eating it up. For what was involved was the cause of your life, the cause of your comrades' lives."

The scientists who carried on Vavilov's work during the siege felt like they were a part of something bigger than themselves. This Just Cause, "a mission for all humanity," as Vavilov called it, gave their work and their lives purpose and meaning beyond any one individual or the very real struggles they faced in the moment of the siege. To have fed themselves or even to have fed the masses of starving residents in the city would have been a finite solution to a finite problem. Though they may have helped prolong the lives of some who would likely still have died or even saved the lives of others, they were looking beyond the immediate horizon. They weren't imagining the relatively few lives they could save in Leningrad; they imagined a future state in which their work might save entire civilizations. Their work was not devoted to getting to the end of the siege; they were playing to keep the human race going for as long as possible.

What a Just Cause Is

Howard's Little League team was one of the, if not the, worst in the league. At the end of each lost game, his coach would say to the players, "It doesn't matter who wins or loses, what matters is how we played the game." At which point, the precocious young Howard would raise his hand and ask the coach, "Then why do we keep score?"

When we play in a finite game, we play the game to win. Even if we hope to simply play well and enjoy the game, we do not play to lose. The motivation to play in an infinite game is completely different—the goal is not to win, but to keep playing. It is to advance something bigger than ourselves or our organizations. And any leader who wishes to lead in the Infinite Game must have a crystal clear Just Cause.

A Just Cause is a specific vision of a future state that does not yet exist; a future state so appealing that people are willing to make sacrifices in order to help advance toward that vision. Like Vavilov's scientists, the sacrifice people are willing to make may be their lives. But it needn't be. It can be the choice to turn down a better-paying job in order to keep working for an organization that is working to advance a Just Cause in which we believe. It may mean working late hours or taking frequent business trips. Though we may not like the sacrifices we make, it is because of the Just Cause that they feel worth it.

"Winning" provides a temporary thrill of victory; an intense, but fleeting, boost to our self-confidence. None of us is able to hold on to the incredible feeling of accomplishment for that target we hit, promotion we earned or tournament we won a year ago. Those feelings have passed. To get that feeling again, we need to try to win again. However, when there is a Just Cause, a reason to come to work that is bigger than any particular win, our days take on more meaning and feel more fulfilling. Feelings that carry on week after week, month after month, year after year. In an organization that is only driven by the finite, we may like our jobs some days, but we will likely never *love* our jobs. If we work for an organization with a Just Cause, we may like our jobs some days, but we will always love our jobs. As with our kids, we may like them some days and not others, but we love them every day.

A Just Cause is not the same as our WHY. A WHY comes from the past. It is an origin story. It is a statement of who we are—the sum total of our values and beliefs. A Just Cause is about the future. It defines where we are going. It describes the world we hope to live in and will commit to help build. Everyone has their own WHY (and everyone can know what their WHY is if they choose to uncover it). But we do not have to have our own Just Cause, we can choose to join someone else's. Indeed we can start a movement, or we can choose to join one and make it our own. Unlike a WHY, of which there can be only one, we can work to advance more than one Just Cause. Our WHY is fixed and it cannot be changed. In contrast, because a Just Cause is about something as of yet unbuilt, we do not know exactly the form it will take. We can work tirelessly to build it however we want and make constant improvements along the way.

Think of the WHY like the foundation of a house, it is the starting point. It gives whatever we build upon it strength and permanence. Our Just Cause is the ideal vision of the house we hope to build. We can work a lifetime to build it and still we will not be finished. However, the results of our work help give the house form. As it moves from our imagination to reality it inspires more people to join the Cause and continue the work . . . forever. For example, my WHY is to inspire people to do what inspires them so that together we can each change our world for the better. It is uniquely mine. My Just Cause is to build a world in which the vast majority of people wake up inspired, feel safe at work and return home fulfilled at the end of the day, and I am looking for as many people as possible who will join me in this Cause.

It is the Just Cause that we are working to advance that gives our work and our lives meaning. A Just Cause inspires us to stay focused beyond the finite rewards and individual wins. The Just Cause provides the context for all the finite games we must play along the way. A Just Cause is what inspires us to want to keep playing. Whether in science, nation building or business, leaders who want us to join them in their infinite pursuit must offer us, in clear terms, an affirmative and tangible vision of the ideal future state they imagine.

When the Founding Fathers of the United States declared independence from Great Britain, for example, they knew that such a radical act would require a statement of Just Cause. "We hold these truths to be self-evident, that all men are created equal," they wrote in the Declaration of Independence, "that they are endowed by their Creator with certain unalienable Rights, that among these are Life, Liberty and the pursuit of

Happiness." The vision they set forth was not simply one of a nation defined by borders but of an ideal future state defined by principles of liberty and equality for all. And on July 4, 1776, the fifty-six men who signed on to that vision agreed to "mutually pledge to each other our Lives, our Fortunes and our sacred Honor." This was how much it mattered to them. They were willing to give up their own finite lives and interests to carry forward the infinite idea and ideals of a new nation. Their sacrifice, in turn, inspired subsequent generations to embrace the same Cause and devote their own blood, sweat and tears to continue to advance it.

We know a Cause is just when we commit to it with the confidence that others will carry on our legacy. This was certainly the case for America's founders. And it was the case for Nikolai Vavilov. Vavilov's vision of a world in which entire populations, and indeed all of humanity, will always have a source of food, ensuring that we can survive as long as possible, carries on to this day. There are nearly two thousand seed banks spread across more than one hundred countries around the world that are continuing the work that Vavilov started a lifetime ago. The Svalbard Global Seed Vault in Norway is one of the largest. Located in a naturally temperature-controlled environment in the Arctic, the Svalbard Vault stores over a billion seeds from nearly six thousand species of flora. It is there to ensure that in the worst-case scenario, we would have a food source to keep our species alive. Marie Haga, the executive director of the Crop Trust, the organization formed in partnership with the United Nations to help support the work of global seed banks, points to Vavilov as the ostensible founder of the cause. "A century after [Vavilov's] first journeys," she said, "a new generation of dedicated crop diversity supporters continue to travel the world to conserve not only germplasm but also Vavilov's legacy."

Many of the organizations we work for now already have some sort of purpose, vision or mission statement (or all of them) written on the walls that our leaders hope will inspire us. However, the vast majority of them would not qualify as a Just Cause. At best they are uninspiring and innocuous, at worst they point us in a direction to keep playing in the finite realm. Even some of the best-intentioned attempts are written in a way that is finite, generic, self-centered or too vague to be of any use in the Infinite Game. Common attempts include statements like, "We do the stuff you don't want to do, so that you can focus on the things that you love to do." It may be a true statement, it's just a true statement for too many things, especially in a business-to-business space. Plus, it's not much of a rallying cry. Another common generic vision sounds like, "To offer the highest quality products at the best possible value, etc., etc." Statements like this are of little use for those who wish to lead us in the Infinite Game. Such statements are not inclusive. They are egocentric—about the company; they look inward and are not about the future state to which the products or services are contributing.

Vizio, the California-based maker of televisions and speakers, says on their website, for example, that they exist to "deliver high performance, smarter products with the latest innovations at a significant savings that we can pass along to our consumers." I take them at their word that they do all those things. But do those words *really* inspire people to want to offer their blood, sweat or tears? When you read those words are you inspired to rush to apply for a job there? Few if any of us get goose bumps or feel a visceral calling to be a part of something like that. Such statements offer us neither a cause to which we would commit ourselves nor a sense of what it's all for, both of which are essential in the Infinite Game.

Again, a Just Cause is a specific vision of a future state that does not yet exist. And in order for a Just Cause to provide direction for our work, to inspire us to sacrifice, and to endure not just in the present but for lifetimes beyond our own, it must meet five standards. Those who are unsure whether their purpose, mission or vision statement is a Just Cause or those interested in leading with a Just Cause can use these standards as a simple test.

A Just Cause must be:

- **For something**—affirmative and optimistic
- **Inclusive**—open to all those who would like to contribute
- **Service oriented**—for the primary benefit of others
- **Resilient**—able to endure political, technological and cultural change
- **Idealistic**—big, bold and ultimately unachievable

For something—affirmative and optimistic

A Just Cause is something we stand for and believe in, not something we oppose. Leaders can rally people *against* something quite easily. They can whip them into a frenzy, even. For our emotions can run hot when we are angry or afraid. Being *for* something, in contrast, is about feeling inspired. Being *for* ignites the human spirit and fills us with hope and optimism. Being *against* is about vilifying, demonizing or rejecting. Being *for* is about inviting all to join in common cause. Being *against* focuses our attention on the things we can see in order to elicit reactions. Being *for* focuses our attention on the unbuilt future in order to spark our imaginations.

Imagine if instead of fighting *against* poverty, for example, we fought *for* the right of every human to provide for their own family. The first creates a common enemy, something we are against. It sets up the Cause as if it is "winnable," i.e., a finite game. It leads us to believe that we can defeat poverty once and for all. The second gives us a cause to advance. The impact of the two perspectives is more than semantics. It affects how we view the problem/vision that affects our ideas on how we can contribute. Where the first offers us a problem to solve, the second offers a vision of possibility, dignity and empowerment. We are not inspired to "reduce" poverty, we are inspired to "grow" the number of people who are able to provide for themselves and their families.

Being for or being against is a subtle but profound difference that the writers of the Declaration of Independence intuitively understood.

Those who led America toward independence stood *against* Great Britain in the short term. Indeed the American colonists were deeply offended by how they were treated by England. Over 60 percent of the Declaration of Independence is spent laying out specific grievances against the king. However, the Cause they were fighting *for* was the true source of lasting inspiration, and in the Declaration of Independence it came before anything else. It is the first idea we read in the document. It sets the context for the rest of the Declaration and the direction for moving forward. It is the ideal to which we personally relate and that we have easily committed to memory. Few Americans, except for scholars and the most zealous of history buffs, can rattle off even one of the complaints listed later in the document, things like: "He has endeavored to prevent the Population of these States; for that purpose obstructing the Laws for naturalization of foreigners; refusing to pass others to encourage their Migrations hither, and raising the Conditions of new Appropriations of Lands." In contrast, most Americans can recite with ease "all men are created equal" and can usually rattle off the three tenets of "Life, Liberty and the pursuit of Happiness." These words are indelibly marked on the cultural psyche. Invoked by patriots and politicians alike, they remind Americans of who we strive to be and the ideals upon which our nation was founded. They tell us what we stand *for*.

Inclusive—open to all those who would like to contribute

Human beings want to feel a part of something. We crave the feeling of belonging. We enjoy the feeling of being part of a group, like when we attend church, attend a parade or rally or wear the jersey of our favorite team when we attend a sports event. A Just Cause serves as an invitation to join others in advancing a cause bigger than ourselves. When the words of the Just Cause help us imagine a positive, specific, alternative vision of the future, it stirs something inside us that makes us want to raise our hand to join up and join in.

A well-crafted statement of Cause inspires us to offer our ideas, our time, our experience, our hands, anything that may help advance the new vision of the future it articulates. This is how movements come to be. It starts with a few people. Their idealized vision of the future attracts believers. Those early adopters don't show up to get anything, they show up to give. They want to help. They want to play a role in advancing toward a new version of the future. The Cause that attracted them becomes their own.

Organizations that simply promise to "change the world" or "make an impact" tell us very little about what specifically they want to accomplish. The sentiments are good, but they are too generic to serve as a meaningful filter for us. Again, a Just Cause is a *specific* vision of a future state that does not yet exist; a future state so appealing that people are willing to make sacrifices in order to help advance toward that vision. We call it "vision" because it must be something we can "see." For a Just Cause to serve as an effective invitation, the words must paint a specific and tangible picture of the kind of impact we will make or what exactly a better world would look like. Only when we can imagine in our mind's eye the exact version of the world an organization or leader hopes to advance toward will we know to which organization or to which leader we want to commit our energies and ourselves. A clear Cause is what ignites our passions.

"We only hire passionate people" is the oft-recited standard of many a person responsible for hiring. How do they know, however, whether the candidate is passionate for interviewing but not so passionate for the Cause? The reality is, EVERYONE is passionate about something, but we aren't all passionate about the same thing. Infinite-minded leaders actively seek out employees, customers and investors who share a passion for the Just Cause. For employees, this is what we mean when we say, "Hire for culture and you can always teach the skills later." For customers and investors, this the root of love and loyalty for the organization itself.

The quick-serve salad company Sweetgreen stands for something bigger than selling salads, for example, and they invite would-be contributors to join their Cause. Their stated mission is "to inspire healthier communities by connecting people to real food." Real food, as Sweetgreen defines it, means ingredients from local sources that support local farms. Which is why their stores have different menus depending on which part of the country they are in. Though many of us may buy their salads just because we like their salads, those who are devoted to locally sourced food and want to support local farms will be drawn to work for and become the most loyal supporters of Sweetgreen. They will make sacrifices, like going out of their way or paying a premium, to buy from Sweetgreen. Supporting the company in some shape or form is one of the things they do to feel that they are advancing their own values and beliefs, their own vision of a better world. They feel included in the Cause.

Service oriented—for the primary benefit of others

A Just Cause must involve at least two parties—the contributors and the beneficiaries. The givers and receivers. Contributors give something, e.g., their ideas, hard work or money, to help advance the Just Cause. And the receivers of those contributions benefit. For a Just Cause to pass the service-orientation test, the primary benefit of the organization's contributions must always go to people other than the contributors themselves.

If my boss offers me career advice, for example, that advice must be for the primary benefit of my career and not theirs. If I am an investor, I must intend that the primary benefit of my contribution goes to helping the company advance its Just Cause. If I am a leader, I must intend that the primary benefit of my time, effort and decisions goes to those I lead. If I am a frontline employee, I must intend that the primary benefit of my efforts goes to the people buying our product or service. If there is only one party, if we are the sole beneficiaries of our work, that's not a Just Cause, that's a vanity project.

When Sweetgreen talks about the beneficiaries of its contributions, they talk about communities and people. They don't talk about what their contributions will do for Sweetgreen. And the drafters of the Declaration of Independence were clear that "We the people," not "We the leaders," would be the primary beneficiaries of their efforts and of the Revolution. If those who led the fight had made themselves the primary beneficiaries, then America probably would have ended up with a dictatorship or an oligarchy. With that new perspective, we instantly see what follows when a company says the primary beneficiaries of their work are shareholders, not customers.

The operative word in all this is "primary." Service orientation does not mean charity. In charity, the vast majority, if not all, the benefit of our contributions must go to the receiver. And any benefit the contributor gets is the good feeling that they contributed. In business, of course we can consider how our work will benefit us or advance our own lot. Of course we can expect and even demand to be fairly compensated and recognized for our efforts and results. We can want our investors to benefit too, just not at the expense of the company, the people who work there or the customers who buy from us. No beneficiary, no customer, should be forced to buy a substandard product and no employee should lose their job as a result of cost cutting performed to benefit a shareholder, who is, after all, just one of a group of contributors. Again, only when the primary beneficiary of the Cause is someone other than the organization itself can the Cause be Just.

This is what "servant leadership" means. It means the primary benefit of the contributions flows downstream. In an organization where service orientation is lacking (or treated as a sideshow rather than the main event), the flow of benefits tends to go upstream instead. Investors invest with the primary intention of seeing a return before anyone else. Leaders make decisions that benefit themselves before those in their charge. Salespeople ensure they do whatever they need to do to make the sale to earn their bonus, regardless of what the customer needs. This is the common flow of benefit in so many of our organizations today. Too many of our cultures are filled with people working to protect their own interests and the interests of those above them before those of the people they are supposed to be serving.

The requirement that a Just Cause be service oriented is consistent with how infinite games are supposed to be played. The infinite player wants to keep the game going for others. A leader who wishes to build an organization equipped for the Infinite Game must never make decisions solely to boost their own compensation. Their efforts should go toward equipping the organization for the game in which it is operating. Even an investor must not be the primary beneficiary of their investment. Rather it is the organization in which they believe and whose Just Cause they want to see advanced that must benefit from their financial contribution. An infinite-minded investor wants to contribute to advance something bigger than themselves—which, if it is successful, will be highly profitable. A finite-minded investor is more like a gambler who bets solely so they may reap the reward. Let us not confuse the two behaviors.

The reason a service orientation is so important in the Infinite Game is because it builds a loyal base of employees and customers (and investors) who will stick with the organization through thick and thin. It is this strong base of loyalty that gives any organization a kind of strength and longevity that money alone cannot provide. The most loyal employees feel their leaders genuinely care about them . . . because their leaders genuinely do care about them. In return, they offer their best ideas, act freely and responsibly and work to solve problems for the benefit of the company. The most loyal customers feel the company genuinely cares about their wants, needs and desires . . . because the company really does. And in return, this is why loyal customers go out of their way or pay a premium to buy from that company over another and encourage their friends to do the same. And the best-led companies feel like their investors genuinely care about helping the company become as strong as possible in order to advance the Cause because the investors really do care. The results benefit all stakeholders.

Resilient—able to endure political, technological and cultural change

Leaders who wish to lead with an infinite mindset would do well to keep the example of the Declaration of Independence in mind. The founders' stated commitment to equality and unalienable human rights are evergreen. Over the course of more than 240 years, even as the nation's leaders, landscape, people and culture have changed, the Just Cause has remained as relevant and inspiring as ever. It is a Just Cause for an infinite time frame.

In the Infinite Game of business, a Just Cause must be greater than the products we make and the services we offer. Our products and services are some of the things we use to advance our Cause. They are not themselves the Cause. If we articulate our Cause in terms of our products, then our organization's entire existence is conditional on the relevance of those products. Any new technology could render our products, our Cause and indeed our entire company obsolete overnight. The American railroads, for example, were some of the largest companies in the country. Until advancements in automotive technology and a network of highways offered people a quicker and sometimes cheaper alternative to the train. Had the railroads defined their need to exist in terms related to moving people and things instead of advancing the railroad, they might be the owners of major car companies or airlines today. Publishers saw themselves in the book business instead of the spreading-ideas business and thus missed the opportunity to capitalize on new technology to advance their cause. They could have invented Amazon or the digital e-reader. Had the music industry defined themselves as the sharers of music rather than sellers of records, tapes and CDs they would have had an easier time in a world of digital streaming. By defining themselves by a cause greater than the products they sold, they could have invented services like iTunes or Spotify. But they didn't . . . and now they are paying the price for it.

Markets will rise and fall, people will come and go, technologies will evolve, products and services will adapt to consumer tastes and market demands. We need something with permanence for us to rally around. Something that can withstand change and crisis. To keep us in the Infinite Game, our Cause must be durable, resilient and timeless.

Idealistic—big, bold and ultimately unachievable

When the signers of the Declaration of Independence affirmed that all men "are created equal" and "endowed . . . with certain unalienable Rights," they were referring primarily to white, Anglo-Saxon, Protestant men. Almost immediately, however, there were efforts to advance a more expansive and inclusive understanding of the ideal. During the Revolutionary War, for example, George Washington forbade anti-Catholic organizing in his armies and regularly attended Catholic services to model the behavior he expected of his men. Nearly a hundred years later, the Civil War brought about an end to slavery, and soon after that the Fourteenth Amendment granted citizenship and equal rights to African Americans and former slaves. The women's suffrage movement took another step toward America's Just Cause when it gained the vote for women in 1920.

The Civil Rights Act of 1964 and the Voting Rights Act of 1965, which protected African Americans and others from discrimination, were two more steps. The nation took yet another step in 2015 with the Supreme Court decision in *Obergefell v. Hodges*, which extended the protections guaranteed by the Fourteenth Amendment to gay marriage.

If the founders of the United States had only set out a goal—to win independence—once it was achieved, they would have grabbed a pint of ale and sat around playing rounds of ninepins and ring taw while regaling each other with how great it was that they won the war. But that's not what happened. Instead, they got to work writing a constitution (which was only fully ratified seven years after the official end of the Revolutionary War) to further codify a set of enduring principles to protect and advance their big, bold, idealistic vision of the future. A vision that Americans have been striving to protect and advance ever since quill and ink touched paper . . . and will continue to protect and advance as long as we have the will and resources to do so. America's Just Cause has yet to be fully realized, and for all practical purposes it never will be. But we will die trying. And that's the point.

Indeed, the abolition of slavery, women's suffrage, the Civil Rights Act and gay rights are some of the big steps the nation has taken to realize its Cause. And though each of those movements, infinite in their own right, are still far from complete, they still represent clear steps along the nation's march toward the ideals enshrined in the Declaration of Independence. It is important to celebrate our victories, but we cannot linger on them. For the Infinite Game is still going and there is still much work to be done. Those victories must serve as milestones of our progress toward an idealized future. They give us a glimpse of what our idealized future can look like and serve as an inspiration to keep moving forward.

This is what the idealized journey of a Just Cause feels like—no matter how much we have achieved, we always feel we have further to go. Think of a Just Cause like an iceberg. All we ever see is the tip of that iceberg, the things we have already accomplished. In an organization, it is often the founders and early contributors who have the clearest vision of the unknown future, of what, to everyone else, remains unseen. The clearer the words of the Just Cause, the more likely they will attract and invite the innovators and early adopters, those willing to take the first risks to advance something that exists almost entirely in their imaginations. With each success, a little more of the iceberg is revealed to others; the vision becomes more visible to others. And when others can see a vision become something real, skeptics become believers and even more people feel inspired by the possibility and willingly commit their time and energy, ideas and talents to help advance the Cause further. But no matter how much of the iceberg we can see, our leaders have the responsibility to remind us that the vast majority still lies unexplored. For no matter how much success we may enjoy, the Just Cause for which we are working lies ahead and not behind.

When You Have Your Cause, Write It Down

The Founding Fathers of the United States were larger-than-life figures. They lived and breathed their Just Cause. This is often the case with inspirational leaders in business as well. But what happens when those charismatic keepers of the Cause move on, retire or die? I am often surprised how many visionary leaders don't think they need to find the words for or write down their Cause. They assume that because their vision is clear to them it's clear to everyone else in the organization. Which of course it's not.

Without finding the words for the Just Cause and writing them down, it dramatically increases the risk that, in time, the Cause will be diluted or disappear altogether. And without the Just Cause, an organization starts to function like a ship without a compass—it veers off course. Focus moves from beyond the horizon to the dials in front of them. Without a Just Cause to guide them, finite-mindedness starts to creep in. The leaders will celebrate how fast they are going or how many miles they have traveled, but fail to recognize that their journey lacks any direction or purpose.

A Just Cause that is preserved on paper can be handed down from generation to generation; a founder's instinct cannot. Like the Declaration of Independence, a written statement of Cause dramatically increases the chances that the Cause will survive to guide and inspire future generations beyond the founders and those who knew the founders. It's the difference between a verbal contract and a written contract. Both are legal and enforceable, but when a contract is written it prevents any confusion or disagreement about the terms of the deal . . . especially for people who weren't there when the deal was made.

A written cause works like a compass. And with a compass in hand, each succession of leaders, their gaze looking beyond the horizon, can more easily navigate the technologies, politics and cultural norms of the day without the founder present.

Chapter 3

CAUSE. NO CAUSE.

Let's play a quick round of Cause. No Cause.

It is a good thing that more and more companies seem to be embracing the importance of having a purpose at the heart of their business. The problem is, too many of them say things that only sound like a Just Cause. Indeed, they may even use language and meet some of the standards of a Just Cause. Until they can check all five boxes, however, what they offer simply isn't a Just Cause.

There are a few main reasons we fail to put forward a true Just Cause. Sometimes, the visionary, Cause-driven leader adopts a false cause by accident because they are struggling to find the words to embody what they imagine for the future (see previous chapter for help). In other cases, the leader wants people to believe that they are Cause driven when, in fact, they have no vision at all. Common "imposter causes" include things like moon shots, a drive to "be the best," or mistaking "growth" for purpose. It is also common to find organizations confusing their corporate social responsibility (CSR) program for a Just Cause. Any of these may or may not work in the finite game, but they absolutely cannot lead an organization to survive and thrive in the Infinite Game.

The reason to identify these pitfalls is first, as a warning, that to embrace any of these will not prepare an organization for life in the Infinite Game, but rather keep it playing squarely with a finite mindset. The other reason to point them out is simply so that we can know if indeed we have a Just Cause or not and go back to the drawing board if we need to. We might even avoid coming up with a false cause in the first place. An organization that has a false cause is not a bad company, it just means they may have a little more work to do. The ability to recognize false causes can also save us pain as investors, employees and consumers. If we suspect that one organization does not have a Just Cause, we can move on to another that does.

A true Just Cause is deeply personal to those who hear it, and it must be deeply personal to those who espouse it. The more personal it is for people, the more likely our passions will be stoked to help advance it. If the words of a Just Cause are used simply to boost a brand image, attract passionate employees or help drive some near-term goal, like a purchase, a vote or support for the company, the impact will be short lived. As soon as we start working at an organization or interacting with its people, we will quickly find out whether they are offering us a Just Cause they truly believe in or just hollow words.

Moon Shots Are Not a Just Cause

He offered us something to believe in. Something that was bigger than us. Something that we were willing to sacrifice to see happen. "We choose to go to the moon," said President John F. Kennedy with determination. "We choose to go to the moon in this decade . . . not because [it is] easy, but because [it is] hard, because that goal will serve to organize and measure the best of our energies and skills, because that challenge is one that we are willing to accept, one we are unwilling to postpone, and one which we intend to win." And just over eight years after Kennedy first challenged the nation, Neil Armstrong took "one small step for a man, one giant leap for mankind."

The so-called moon shot is often invoked by leaders who are trying to inspire their people to reach for something that seems impossible. And because moon shots pass most of the tests of a Just Cause, it usually works. In the case of Kennedy's actual moon shot, it is affirmative and specific. It is inclusive, service oriented and definitely worthy of sacrifice. However, it is not infinite. No matter how hard the challenge, no matter how impossible it seemed, the moon shot was an achievable, finite goal. More than an ideal future state, it is what Jim Collins, author of *Good to Great* and *Built to Last*, calls a BHAG, a big, hairy, audacious goal. It's easy to mistake a BHAG for a Just Cause because they can indeed be incredibly inspiring and can often take many years to achieve. But after the moon shot has been achieved the game continues. Simply choosing another big, audacious goal is not infinite play, it's just another finite pursuit.

During employee town hall meetings at GE, some of the employees would express concern that the company was too focused on the short term. Jack Welch, then CEO, was fond of replying, "Long term is just a series of short terms." When employees express such a concern to a CEO, more likely than not what they are really asking is: "What's this all for?" What is all our hard work contributing to beyond the metrics and material rewards? Welch's answer revealed that, to him, there was no higher cause at play. The goal was simply to perform, perform again and perform again. To Welch, each finite accomplishment was enough. Except, business is an infinite game, which means the series of short terms never ends.

Indeed, leaping from goal to goal can be fun for a while, but if that's all there is, over time the thrill of each achievement becomes less, well, thrilling. I often meet senior executives who seem to suffer from a kind of "finite exhaustion." Because they did well and were paid well for hitting each goal set for them, they kept repeating that pattern. At some point in their careers, they traded any fantasy of feeling like their work would contribute to something bigger than themselves for a rat race or a hamster wheel or some other unfulfilling running rodent metaphor. Racking up finite wins does not lead to something more infinite.

The question that a Just Cause must answer is: What is the infinite and lasting vision that a moon shot will help advance? A Just Cause is the context for all our other goals, big and small, and all of our finite achievements must help to advance the Just Cause. Indeed, if we become overly concerned with a finite goal, no matter how inspiring, we leave ourselves open to making decisions that are only good for the finite but may do damage to the infinite.

Kennedy's moon shot was made in the context of the larger infinite vision that America's Founding Fathers laid out—that our progress is not for the benefit of a few, but for the benefit of many. In the sentences before Kennedy proposed his moon shot challenge, he offered the infinite context for the finite objective, "We set sail on this new sea because there is new knowledge to be gained, and new rights to be won, and they must be won and used for the progress of all people." This was his belief for a good many of his objectives, including landing a man on the moon and returning him home safely.

Though moon shots are inspiring for a time, that inspiration comes with an expiration date. Moon shots are bold, inspiring finite goals *within* the Infinite Game, not *instead* of the Infinite Game.

Being the Best Is Not a Just Cause

"We will be the global leader in every market we serve and our products will be sought after for their compelling design, superior quality, and best value." This is a pretty typical-sounding corporate vision or mission statement. This one belongs to Garmin, the maker of GPS devices for everyone from runners to pilots. Though there are dozens of variations, the basic formula is the same— we're the best and everyone wants our products because our products are the best . . . and "they're great value" (gotta squeeze that in).

Again, vision or mission statements act like compasses. They guide our direction. However, because there are no standards on how to write such statements, ones like the above have become too common. Broad and generic, they offer little to no value to a company that wants to adopt an infinite mindset. "Being the best" and statements like that are egocentric statements that place the company as the primary subject (and thus the primary beneficiary) of their vision. They don't help make the company relevant to those who buy from the company. In fact, any mention of the customer or any offer of value usually comes at the end of the statement. By putting the egocentric statement first, it directs leaders to focus their efforts inward and not on actual people who may buy the product. And just because people may buy or like the product does not mean they believe in or even know what the Cause is.

Leaders with a finite mindset often confuse having a successful product with having a strong company. Which is a little like the owners of the Los Angeles Lakers thinking their team is relevant because LeBron James has relevance. Having a great player, a popular product or a killer app does not mean we are equipped for the Infinite Game. Vision statements that place the product at the center of the vision are only useful so long as nothing better ever comes along, there is never a deviation in market conditions and no new technology is ever invented. If, however, any of these things does happen, the company will be left with a vision statement that often leaves them clinging on to an old business model and blind to the opportunities they could have captured. This seems to be what happened to Garmin.

In 2007, Garmin may have been "the best," the global leader in dash-mounted GPS units for cars and boats. However, as smartphones became more reliable and more capable, we had less need for a separate GPS unit anymore and the company suffered as a result. It is now worth less than a third of what it was worth in 2007. It's too easy for Garmin to simply blame the rise and ubiquity of smartphones to explain their losses (which they did). What they failed to recognize is that they had a vision statement that directed them to focus on their product, and in so doing, they missed the opportunity that smartphones offered them. Had they been obsessing about how to provide the value to customers first, they may have seized the chance to develop the go-to navigation app for mobile phones when the opportunity still existed. Their brand was certainly strong enough to do so. Instead, they continued to focus on the business model they had selling dash-mounted hardware. Now the default navigation apps on our phones are Google Maps, Waze or Apple Maps, but that didn't have to be. A Just Cause should direct the business model, not the other way around.

When a statement of vision or mission is grounded in the product, it can have adverse effects on the corporate culture also. For companies that place their product above all else, which is fairly common among technology or engineering companies, it leaves people who are not engineers or product designers feeling like (and sometimes actually treated like) second-class citizens in their own companies. An organization is better served if everyone, including those in accounting, support or customer service roles, for example, is made to feel like they are not just there to serve the needs of the engineers or product development teams. They too want to feel like valuable members of the team, working together to advance something bigger than the product or themselves.

Being the best simply cannot be a Just Cause, because even if we are the best (based on the metrics and time frames of our own choosing), the position is only temporary. The game doesn't end once we get there; it keeps going. And because the game keeps going, we often find ourselves playing defense to maintain our cherished ranking. Though saying "we are the best" may be great fodder for a rah-rah speech to rally a team, it makes for a weak foundation upon which to build an entire company. Infinite-minded leaders understand that "best" is not a permanent state. Instead, they strive to be "better." "Better" suggests a journey of constant improvement and makes us feel like we are being invited to contribute our talents and energies to make progress in that journey. "Better," in the Infinite Game, is better than "best."

Growth Is Not a Just Cause

Imagine you walk out of your house one morning and see your neighbor packing up his car. "Where are you going?" you ask. "Vacation," he replies. "Nice. Where are you going?" you follow up, curious. "I told you, vacation," he replies again. "I got that," you say, "but *where* are you going?" Exasperated, your neighbor replies again, "I told you, VAY-CAY-SHUN!"

Realizing that your line of questioning will not reveal the answer you're looking for, you try a new strategy. "Okay," you say, "how do you plan to get to your vacation?" And immediately your neighbor offers their plan. "I'm going to drive down the I-90 and my goal is to drive three hundred miles per day."

If the question asked is, "What is your company's Cause? Why does your company exist?" and the answer offered is "growth," that's a lot like your neighboring responding "vacation" to the question "Where are you going?" The leaders of these growth-oriented companies can rattle off their strategies and targets for growth, but that's like explaining which highway and how many miles you plan to travel when heading on vacation; it doesn't paint a picture of why you set off in the first place or where you hope to go. It doesn't offer a larger context or purpose for that growth.

Money is the fuel to advance a Cause, it is not a Cause itself. The reason to grow is so that we have more fuel to advance the Cause. Just as we don't buy a car simply so we can buy more gas, so too must companies offer more value than their ability to make money. A company, like a car, is more valuable to all constituents when it takes us somewhere to which we would otherwise be unable to go. That place we envision going to is the Just Cause.

It's worth noting that so many of the goals that companies put forward tend to be arbitrary or overly ambitious. Especially in the start-up world, the drive for billion-dollar valuations is not an indicator of a healthy company that is built to last. It is a standard that has evolved thanks to the venture capital industry (because valuations are how they make their money). A strong culture and the ability to fund its own existence (also known as profitability) is how a company actually stays in the game for the long term. In addition, the constant drive for hypergrowth creates a problem within mature markets—markets in which the product, technology or business is no longer new or special, but accepted and ubiquitous. For companies in those markets, companies like Sears or GE, their options are unattractive if they maintain a growth-at-all-costs mentality. Many start to play defense, give their money away to shareholders to court their favor or over use stock buybacks to keep their stock price artificially inflated. Growth through acquisition or merger often becomes the only way mature, finite-minded companies can continue to demonstrate high rates of growth. This may win a short-term boost in the stock market; however, as *Harvard Business Review* and many others have reported, "70%–90% of acquisitions are abysmal failures."

To offer growth as a cause, growth for its own sake, is like eating just to get fat. It pushes executives to consider strategies that demonstrate growth with little to no consideration of any sense of purpose for that growth. Just like it would affect a human being, it should come as no surprise that the organizations that eat to get fat will eventually suffer from health problems. Growth as a cause often results in an unhealthy culture, one in which short-termism and selfishness reign supreme, while trust and cooperation suffer. Growth is a result, not a Cause. It's an output, not a reason for being. When we have a Just Cause, we are willing to sacrifice our interests to advance it. When we think money or growth is the Cause, we are more likely to sacrifice others or the Cause itself to protect our interests. Besides, nothing can grow forever. All balloons and bubbles eventually burst . . . even financial ones.

Corporate Social Responsibility Is Not a Just Cause

The company advertised all the good they did in the community. They shared the stories of some of the people who benefited from the scholarships they funded, for example. They wanted their customers and their employees to know they cared about people. Which would have been great if the 60,000 people who actually worked for the company didn't have to work in such a top-heavy, dog-eat-dog toxic culture.

A corporate social responsibility (CSR) program is not a Just Cause. And a company is not cause driven because they sponsor walkathons, donate to charity or give employees paid time off to volunteer. Nor are they cause driven because they give away their products to people who can't afford them.

CSR programs are, for the most part, business-speak for giving to charity. And though having a CSR program is indeed great and commendable, unless you're a charity, it's only a piece of what a company does. The CSR program must be part of the broader strategy to advance the Just Cause. A strategy that includes everything the company does. The way a company makes its money and the way it gives it away must both contribute to advancing the Just Cause. "Cause-related work" is not something an organization does on the side; it is core to their very being. Service is not an ornament. It is a touchstone. And no amount of corporate social responsibility is enough to offset or balance the excessive finite focus that may consume the rest of the corporate culture.

Even well-intended finite-minded leaders often have the perspective of "make money to do good." An infinite perspective on service, however, looks somewhat different: "Do good making money" (the order of the information matters). I will do good in how I treat people and serve my community throughout my life and still build a financially strong organization. It is not so much an equation as it is a lifestyle. These individuals and companies work to be stewards of the lives of those who work for them and for the communities in which they operate. The giving that happens during and at the end of their lives looks more like a continuation of what they've been doing for decades rather than an attempt at balancing the past. The difference is determined by the leaders' mindset.

Chapter 4

KEEPER OF THE CAUSE

S am Walton founded Walmart in 1962 with a simple idea—to serve the average workin' American by offering "the lowest prices anytime, anywhere." At the end of his life, Walton described his vision this way: "If we work together, we'll lower the cost of living for everyone . . . we'll give the world an opportunity to see what it's like to save and have a better life." With Walton at the helm, the decisions that went into building Walmart—from where to locate the stores to how big they would be—were all made with this Cause at the forefront. And as a result, people *loved* Walmart—both those who worked there and those who shopped in their stores. People wanted Walmart stores in their communities. The business grew, and Walton, who had grown up during the Depression, became one of the richest men in America.

And then, somewhere along the way, the Just Cause went fuzzy. By the time Mike Duke took over as CEO in 2009, it was clear that it was no longer the driving force behind the company. Indeed, Walton's original vision was now little more than marketing slogans and hollow words written on the office walls. The company had become obsessed with profit, growth and dominance at the expense of the very Cause that drove their success in the first place.

Mike Duke earned a reputation at Walmart for being an expert in efficiency. When it was announced that Duke would be the next CEO, his predecessor, H. Lee Scott Jr., stammered, "I kind of thought—and I think the board thought—that the company could be better managed." He went on to explain, "Mike is not only a good leader but a really good manager. . . . I don't think in business you can forget the fact that you don't just have to lead, you have to manage." If the board was hoping to correct management issues or enhance performance, then giving a man like Mike Duke the reins might have been a perfect choice . . . for the short term. But if the board was concerned that Sam Walton's Just Cause had been diluted, then a man like Mike Duke was about the worst person to get the company back on track.

Duke's own words when he accepted the position revealed the kind of mindset with which he was going to lead. "[Walmart] is very well positioned in today's economy, growing market share and returns, and is more relevant to its customers than ever," he said in the press release announcing his new role. "Our strategy is sound and our management team is extremely capable. I am confident we will continue to deliver value to our shareholders, increase opportunity for our over 2 million associates, and help our 180 million customers around the world save money and live better."

Notice the order of the information? Duke's first thought was growing market share and returns. Though he talks about being relevant to customers he doesn't actually mention delivering value to them until the end of his statement. It's a strange quirk of human nature. The order in which a person presents information more often than not reveals their actual priorities and the focus of their strategies. Where Sam Walton started with the people's interests, Mike Duke started with Wall Street's.

Under Duke's leadership, Walmart's stock price did increase . . . for a while. However, focusing on numbers before people comes at a cost. The once beloved brand also found itself embroiled in multiple scandals over the treatment of their people and their customers. In 2011, Walmart was the target of one of the largest employment discrimination class action suits ever filed, brought by female employees who claimed they were victims of systematic underpayment and underpromotion. In 2012, there were walkouts and protests by workers who demanded to be treated with dignity and respect and paid a livable wage. Where before communities would rally to bring a Walmart into their neighborhoods, now they were rallying to keep them out. The company's plans for expansion in Denver and New York, for example, were halted by mass protests. There was also a congressional investigation into allegations that Walmart bribed foreign officials to court favor abroad. Needless to say, morale at the company plummeted and much of the love people had for the stores was replaced with contempt.

What happened at Walmart happens all too often in public companies, even the Cause-driven ones. Under pressure from Wall Street, we too often put finite-minded executives in the highest leadership position when what we actually need is a visionary, infinite-minded leader. Steve Ballmer, as we've already discussed, was one such example. John Sculley, who replaced Steve Jobs at Apple in 1983, was another. Instead of trying to continue advancing the Cause, Sculley was more focused on competing head-to-head against IBM. The damage he did to the culture seriously hurt Apple's ability to innovate. In 2000, after being passed over for the CEO job at GE, Robert Nardelli took over at Home Depot (his nickname at GE was "Little Jack," because of how much he emulated and hoped to succeed Jack Welch as CEO). His relentless drive for cost cutting all but destroyed a culture of innovation at Home Depot. In 2004, the COO, Kevin Rollins, replaced Michael Dell to become CEO of Dell. Focused on growth, he presided over the largest layoffs in the company history, a rise in customer complaints and an SEC investigation over accounting issues. These men were all skilled executives. However, their finite mindsets left them ill qualified for the job they had been given. In fact, Sculley at Apple and Rollins at Dell did such damage to their respective organizations that their more infinite-minded predecessors, Steve Jobs and Michael Dell, were brought back to try to repair the messes they made. The problem isn't how skilled an executive is when they take over as CEO. The problem is whether they have the right mindset for the job they are given.

We Need a New Title

The responsibility of every C-level executive is baked into their title. Chief FINANCIAL Officer. Chief MARKETING Officer. Chief TECHNOLOGY Officer. Chief OPERATING Officer. What they are required to do, what they are required to oversee, is right there in their title. One of the things that title does is to help ensure that we put the right person in the right job. Few would ever consider someone who hates numbers and has never been able to understand a balance sheet for a CFO position. And if you find technology confusing and still have that old VCR connected to your TV at home, odds are you're not on any short list to be a CTO anytime soon. So it begs the question, what exactly is a Chief EXECUTIVE Officer?

The lack of a clear standard for the role and responsibilities of the CEO in our organizations is one of the reasons we find too many leaders of companies playing the finite game when they should at least be thinking about the Infinite Game. In too many cases, it's that their title hasn't properly set them up for the job they have. The word "executive" doesn't tell us what a CEO is responsible for.

Words matter. They give direction and meaning to things. Pick the wrong words, intentions change and things won't necessarily go as hoped or expected. Martin Luther King Jr. gave the "I have a dream" speech, for example. He didn't give the "I have a plan" speech. There is no doubt he needed a plan. We know he had meetings to discuss the plan. But as the "CEO" of the civil rights movement, Dr. King was not responsible for making the plan. He was responsible for the dream and making sure those responsible for the plans were working to advance the dream.

General Lori Robinson, who, when she retired from the Air Force in 2018, was the highest-ranking female officer in the history of the United States military, explains that the responsibility of the most senior person in an organization is to look beyond the organization. "I

will go up and out. I need you to go down and in" is how
she framed her responsibility every time she took a new
command. If the top person needs to focus on "up and
out," then we need their title to help frame their primary
responsibility.

Leaders in the Infinite Game will be better equipped
to fulfill their responsibilities if they understand that
they are stepping into the role of a "Chief Vision Officer,"
or CVO. That is the primary job of the person who sits at
the pointy end of the spear. They are the holder,
communicator and protector of the vision. Their job is to
ensure that all clearly understand the Just Cause and
that all other C-level executives direct their efforts to
advancing the Cause inside the organization. It's not that
an infinite-minded leader is entirely unconcerned with
the organization's finite interests. Rather, as the keeper
of the Cause, they take accountability for deciding when
short-term finite costs are worth it to advance the
infinite vision. They think beyond the bottom line. As the
ultimate infinite player, the CVO must go up and out.

Next in Line for the Top Job

In too many of our companies today, we organize around
a single line of hierarchy. The CEO is the number one job
and CFO or COO are usually seen as number two. And in
the vast majority of businesses, most CFOs or COOs see
themselves in line for the "top job." Michael Dinkins,
who worked at GE for 17 years under Jack Welch,
explained:

> I think one of the reasons why a lot of CFOs are
> being elevated to the CEO role is because the CFO
> is one of the few positions that sees the total
> company. Everything that's going on within the
> company. . . . They understand processes within
> the company and the time frame of these processes
> to happen. . . . They see how HR is recruiting. . . .
> They see how a manufacturing plant is going to
> introduce new equipment. . . . They understand the

quality control systems that are over the business. . . . They see the whole company and there's an advantage to that.

Mr. Dinkins's statement makes sense if we are looking for tactical, finite-minded leadership. But not if what we need is a CVO. A CVO is not an operations or a finance job. Whereas CVOs focus on up and out, CFOs and COOs focus on down and in. One requires eyes on the infinite horizon, the other requires eyes on the business plan. One envisions the very distant, abstract future. The other sees the steps to take in the tangible near term.

This is one of the reasons the best organizations are often run in tandem. The combination of the keeper of the vision (CVO) and the operator (the CFO or COO). It is a partnership of complementary skill sets. We are more likely to get these partnerships if we adjust the formal hierarchies in our companies to promote the right mindset to fit the purpose of the job. This means that we need to stop seeing the CEO as number one and the CFO or COO as number two and start thinking of them as vital partners in a common cause. One does not know how to do the other's job better than they do (which is why they need each other). Remember, Steve Ballmer, John Sculley and Kevin Rollins all thrived when they were working alongside their more infinite-minded partners.

Though the CVO is more often in the spotlight, and though the CVO is often given more of the praise, publicly at least, both players must have the strength of ego to know it is a trusted partnership. The CVO knows they cannot advance their vision alone and need someone like Michael Dinkins described by their side. The COO or CFO knows that their skills can work to vastly greater scale and meaning if they are applied to help advance an infinite Just Cause; something bigger than themselves or the company. Such a model has precedence. In the military there are officers and enlisted ranks who work alongside each other. To rise in the enlisted ranks is a different trajectory than a rise in the officer ranks. They are entirely different career paths. There is no conflict of interest when they work together because the most senior enlisted leader on a base cannot aspire to take the job of the most senior officer, and vice versa. When these partnerships work, the CVO and the COO or the CFO spend more time thanking and celebrating each other than competing for attention.

An uncomfortable truth for many CFOs or COOs is that they have already reached the top level of their skill set. They are already the most senior, most skilled finance or operations people in the organization, which is a great thing. Without them, the CVO would not be able to advance the vision. But that doesn't mean that they are equipped to be at the forefront, leading that vision. For many, once they get the "top job" they are more likely to continue doing what they know and do well—thinking about how big they want their companies to be and what kinds of margins, EBITDA, EPS or market share they aim to achieve (finite pursuits)—than they are to embrace the new responsibility of imagining what the future could look like and how the company might advance a Just Cause (an infinite pursuit).

It's like a salesperson who is promoted to sales manager. They might have excelled at making sales, but they are no longer responsible for selling; they are now responsible for taking care of the people who do the selling. If they fail to shift gears, adjust their mindset and learn a new set of skills for their new responsibility, problems will ensue. Any CFO, COO or other executive can absolutely succeed as CVO if they also learn to adapt to their new role and new responsibilities and embrace an infinite mindset. If they fail to do so, they will likely default to the skills that got them their previous job, which increases the probability that they will steer the company down a very finite path.

Whether or not he was qualified to be CVO of Walmart, Duke failed to adjust for the role he was given —he failed to champion Sam Walton's vision into the next century. In contrast, Duke's successor, Doug McMillon, could prove to be the CVO that Walmart needs. When his new position was announced in 2013, McMillon said in a press release, "The opportunity to lead Walmart is a great privilege. Our company has a rich history of delivering value to customers across the globe and, as their needs grow and change, we will be there to serve them. Our management team is talented and experienced, and our strategy gives me confidence that our future is bright. By keeping our promise to customers, we will drive shareholder value, create opportunity for our associates and grow our business." McMillon presented his priorities in literally the exact opposite order that Mike Duke had when he stepped up to lead the company five years earlier. McMillon put Sam Walton's vision first. It is exciting to see how he is reequipping Walmart to once again play in the Infinite Game.

Chapter 5

THE RESPONSIBILITY OF BUSINESS (REVISED)

Business today is subject to a dizzying rate of change. And all that change seems to be taking its toll. The time it takes before a company is forced out of the game is getting shorter and shorter. The average life of a company in the 1950s, if you recall, was just over 60 years. Today it is less than 20 years. According to a 2017 study by Credit Suisse, disruptive technology is the reason for the steep decline in company life span. However, disruptive technologies are not a new phenomenon. The credit card, the microwave oven, Bubble Wrap, Velcro, transistor radio, television, computer hard disks, solar cells, optic fiber, plastic and the microchip were all introduced in the 1950s. Save for Velcro and Bubble Wrap (which are disruptive in a completely different way), that's a pretty good list of disruptive technologies. "Disruption" is likely not the cause of the challenge, it's a symptom of a more insidious root cause. It is not technology that explains failure; it is less about technology, per se, and more about the leaders' failure to envision the future of their business as the world changes around them. It is the result of shortsightedness. And shortsightedness is an inherent condition of leaders who play with a finite mindset. In fact, the rise of this kind of shortsightedness over the past 50 years can be traced back to the philosophies of a single person.

In a watershed article from 1970, Milton Friedman, the Nobel Prize–winning economist, who is considered one of the great theorists of today's form of capitalism, laid out the foundation for the theory of shareholder primacy that is at the heart of so much finite-minded business practice today. "In a free-enterprise, private-property system," he wrote, "a corporate executive is an employee of the owners of the business. He has direct responsibility to his employers. That responsibility is to conduct the business in accordance with their desires, which generally will be to make as much money as possible while conforming to the basic rules of the society, both those embodied in law and those embodied in ethical custom." Indeed, Friedman insisted that "there is one and only one social responsibility of business, to use its resources and engage in activities designed to increase its profits so long as it stays within the rules of the game." In other words, according to Friedman, the sole purpose of business is to make money and that money belongs to shareholders. These ideas are now firmly ingrained in the zeitgeist. Today it is so generally accepted that the "owner" of a company sits at the top of the benefit food chain and that business exists solely to create wealth, that we often assume that this was always the way that the game of business was played and is the only way it can be played. Except it wasn't . . . and it isn't.

Friedman seemed to have a very one-dimensional view of business. And as anyone who has ever led, worked for or bought from a business knows, business is dynamic and complicated. Which means, it is possible that, for the past 40+ years, we have been building companies with a definition of business that is actually bad for business and undermines the very system of capitalism it proclaims to embrace.

Capitalism Before Friedman

For a more infinite-minded alternative to Friedman's definition of the responsibility of business, we can go back to Adam Smith. The eighteenth-century Scottish philosopher and economist is widely accepted as the father of economics and modern capitalism. "Consumption," he wrote in *The Wealth of Nations*, "is the sole end and purpose of all production and the interest of the producer ought to be attended to, only so far as it may be necessary for promoting that of the consumer." He went on to explain, "The maxim is so perfectly self-evident, that it would be absurd to attempt to prove it." Put simply, the company's interests should always be secondary to the interest of the consumer (ironically, a point Smith believed so "self-evident," he felt it was absurd to try to prove it, and yet here I am writing a whole book about it).

Smith, however, was not blind to our finite predilections. He recognized that "in the mercantile system the interest of the consumer is almost constantly sacrificed to that of the producer; and it seems to consider production, and not consumption, as the ultimate end and object of all industry and commerce." In a nutshell, Smith accepted that it was human nature for people to act to advance their own interests. He called our propensity for self-interest the "invisible hand." He went on to theorize that because the invisible hand was a universal truth (because of our selfish motivations we all want to build strong companies), it ultimately benefits the consumer. "It is not from the benevolence of the butcher, the brewer, or the baker that we can expect our dinner, but from their regard to their own interest," he explained. The butcher has a selfish desire to offer the best cuts of meat without regard for the brewer or the baker. And the brewer wants to make the best beer, regardless of what meat or bread is available on the market. And the baker wants to make the tastiest loaves without any consideration for what we may put on our sandwiches. The result, Smith believed, is that we, the consumers, get the best of everything . . . at least we do if the system is balanced. However, Smith did not consider a time in which the selfishness of outside investors and an analyst community would put that system completely out of balance. He did not anticipate that an entire group of self-interested outsiders would exert massive pressure on the baker to cut costs and use cheaper ingredients in order to maximize the investors' gains.

If history or 18th-century brogue-tongued philosophers are not your jam, we need simply look at how capitalism changed after the idea of shareholder supremacy took over—which only happened in the final decades of the twentieth century. Prior to the introduction of the shareholder primacy theory, the way business operated in the United States looked quite different. "By the middle of the 20th century," said Cornell corporate law professor Lynn Stout in the documentary series *Explained*, "the American public corporation was proving itself one of the most effective and powerful and beneficial organizations in the world." Companies of that era allowed for average Americans, not just the wealthiest, to share in the investment opportunities and enjoy good returns. Most important, "executives and directors viewed themselves as stewards or trustees of great public institutions that were supposed to serve not just the shareholders, but also bondholders, suppliers, employees and the community." It was only after Friedman's 1970 article that executives and directors started to see themselves as responsible to their "owners," the shareholders, and not stewards of something bigger. The more that idea took hold in the 1980s and '90s, the more incentive structures inside public companies and banks themselves became excessively focused on shorter-and-shorter-term gains to the benefit of fewer and fewer people. It's during this time that the annual round of mass layoffs to meet arbitrary projections became an accepted and common strategy for the first time. Prior to the 1980s, such a practice simply didn't exist. It was common for people to work a practical lifetime for one company. The company took care of them and they took care of the company. Trust, pride and loyalty flowed in both directions. And at the end of their careers these long-time employees would get their proverbial gold watch. I don't think getting a gold watch is even a thing anymore. These days, we either leave or are asked to leave long before we would ever earn one.

Capitalism Abuse

The finite-minded form of capitalism that exists today bears little resemblance to the more infinite-minded form that inspired America's founders (Thomas Jefferson owned all three volumes of Smith's *Wealth of Nations*) and served as the bedrock for the growth of the American nation. Capitalism today is, in name only, the capitalism that Adam Smith envisioned over 200 years ago. And it looks nothing like the capitalism practiced by companies like Ford, Kodak and Sears in the late 19th and early 20th centuries, before they too fell prey to finite thinking and lost their way. What many leaders in business practice these days is more of an abuse of capitalism, or "capitalism abuse." Like in the case of alcohol abuse, "abuse" is defined as improper use of something. To use something for a reason other than that for which it was intended. And if capitalism was intended to benefit the consumer and the leaders of companies were to be the stewards of something greater than themselves, they are not using it that way today.

Some may say my view—that the purpose of a company is not just to make money but to pursue a Just Cause—is naïve and anticapitalist. First, I would urge us all to beware the messenger. My assumption is that those who most fiercely defend Friedman's views on business, and many of the current and accepted business practices he inspired, are the ones who benefit most from them. But business was never just about making money. As Henry Ford said, "A business that makes nothing but money is a poor kind of business." Companies exist to advance something—technology, quality of life or anything else with the potential to ease or enhance our lives in some way, shape or form. That people are willing to pay money for whatever a company has to offer is simply proof that they perceive or derive some value from those things. Which means the more value a company offers, the more money and the more fuel they will have for further advancements. Capitalism is about more than prosperity (measured in features and benefits, dollars and cents); it's also about progress (measured in quality of life, technological advancements and the ability of the human race to live and work together in peace).

The constant abuse since the late 1970s has left us with a form of capitalism that is now, in fact, broken. It is a kind of bastardized capitalism that is organized to advance the interests of a few people who abuse the system for personal gain, which has done little to advance the true benefits of capitalism as a philosophy (as evidenced by anticapitalist and protectionist movements around the globe). Indeed, the entire philosophy of shareholder primacy and Friedman's definition of the purpose of business was promoted by investors themselves as a way to incentivize executives to prioritize and protect their finite interests above all else.

It is due in large part to Milton Friedman's ideas, for example, that corporations started tying executive pay to short-term share price performance rather than the long-term health of the company. And those who embraced Friedman's views rewarded themselves handsomely. The Economic Policy Institute reported that in 1978, the average CEO made approximately 30 times the average worker's salary. By 2016, the average had increased over 800 percent to 271 times the average worker's pay. Where the average CEO has seen a nearly 950 percent increase in their earnings, the American worker, meanwhile, has seen just over 11 percent in theirs. According to the same report, average CEO pay has increased at a rate 70 percent faster than the stock market!

It doesn't take an MBA to understand why. As Dr. Stout explains in her book, *The Shareholder Value Myth*, "If 80 percent of the CEO's pay is based on what the share price is going to do next year, he or she is going to do their best to make sure that share price goes up, even if the consequences might be harmful to employees, to customers, to society, to the environment or even to the corporation itself in the long-term." When we tie pay packages directly to stock price, it promotes practices like closing factories, keeping wages down, implementing extreme cost cutting and conducting annual rounds of layoffs—tactics that might boost the stock price in the near term, but often do damage to an organization's ability to survive and thrive in the Infinite Game. Buybacks are another often legitimate practice that has been abused by public company executives seeking to prop up their share price. By buying back its own shares, based on the laws of supply and demand, they temporarily increase demand for their stock, which temporarily drives up the price (which temporarily makes the executives look good).

Though many of the practices used to drive up stock prices in the short term sound ethically dubious, if we look back to Friedman's definition of the responsibility of business, we find that he leaves the door wide open for such behavior, even encourages it. Remember, his only guidance for the responsibility companies must obey is to act within the bounds of the law and "ethical custom." I, as one observer, am struck by that awkward phrase, "ethical custom." Why not just say "ethics"? Does ethical custom mean that if we do something frequently enough it becomes normalized and is thus no longer unethical? If so many companies use regular rounds of mass layoffs, using people's livelihoods, to meet arbitrary projections, does that strategy then cease to be unethical? If everyone is doing it, it must be okay.

As a point of fact, laws and "ethical customs" usually come about in response to abuses, not by predicting them. In other words, they always lag behind. Based on the common interpretation of Friedman's definition, it's almost a requirement for companies to exploit those gaps to maximize profit until future laws and ethical customs tell them they can't. Based on Friedman, it is their responsibility to do so!

Technology companies, like Facebook, Twitter and Google, certainly look like they are more comfortable asking for forgiveness as they run afoul of ethical customs, as opposed to leading with a fundamental view of how they safeguard one of their most important assets: our private data. Based on Friedman's standards, they are doing exactly what they should do.

If we are using a flawed definition of business to build our companies today, then we are likely also promoting people and forming leadership teams best qualified to play by the finite rules that Friedman espoused—leadership teams that are probably the least equipped to navigate the ethical requirements necessary to avoid exploiting the system for self-gain. Built with the wrong goal in mind, these teams are more likely to make decisions that do long-term damage to the very organizations, people and communities they are supposed to be leading and protecting. As King Louis XV of France said in 1757, "*Après moi le dèluge.*" "After me comes the flood." In other words, the disaster that will follow after I'm gone will be your problem, not mine. A sentiment that seems to be shared by too many finite leaders today.

The Pressure to Play with a Finite Mindset

It's a big open secret among the vast majority of public-company executives that the theory of shareholder primacy and the pressure Wall Street exerts on them are actually bad for business. The great folly is that despite this knowledge and their private grumblings and misgivings, they continue to defend the principle and yield to the pressure.

I am not going to waste precious ink making a drawn-out argument about the long-term impact of what happened to our country and global economies when executives bowed to those pressures. It is enough to call attention to the man-made recession of 2008, the increasing stress and insecurity too many of us feel at work and a gnawing feeling that too many of our leaders care more about themselves than they do about us. This is the great irony. The defenders of finite-minded capitalism act in a way that actually imperils the survival of the very companies from which they aim to profit. It's as if they have decided that the best strategy to get the most cherries is to chop down the tree.

Thanks in large part to the loosening of regulations that were originally introduced to prevent banks from wielding the kind of influence and speculative tendencies that caused the Great Depression of 1929 to happen, investment banks once again wield massive amounts of power and influence. The result is obvious—Wall Street forces companies to do things they shouldn't do and discourages them from doing things they should.

Entrepreneurs are not immune from the pressure either. In their case, there is often intense pressure to demonstrate constant, high-speed growth. To achieve that goal, or when growth slows, they turn to venture capital or private equity firms to raise money. Which sounds good in theory. Except there is a flaw in the business model of private equity that can wreak havoc with any company keen to stay in the game. For private equity and venture capital firms to make money, they have to sell. And it's often about three to five years after they make their initial investment. A private equity firm or venture capitalist can use all the flowery, infinite game, Cause-focused language they want. And they may believe it. Up until the point they have to sell. And then all of a sudden many will care a lot less about the Just Cause and all the other stakeholders. The pressure investors can exert on the company to do things in the name of finite objectives can be and often is devastating to the long-term prospects of the company. Long is the list of purpose-driven executives who say that *their* investors are different, that they *do* care about the company's Cause . . . until it's time to sell. (The ones I talked to asked that I not mention the names of their companies for fear of upsetting their investors.)

There is no such thing as constant growth, nor is there any rule that says high-speed growth is necessarily a great strategy when building a company to last. Where a finite-minded leader sees fast growth as the goal, an infinite-minded leader views growth as an adjustable variable. Sometimes it is important to strategically slow the rate of growth to help ensure the security of the long-term or simply to make sure the organization is properly equipped to withstand the additional pressures that come with high-speed growth. A fast-growing retail operation, for example, may choose to slow the store expansion schedule in order to put more resources into training and development of staff and store managers. Opening stores is not what makes a company successful; having those stores operate well is. It's in a company's interest to get things done right now rather than wait to deal with the problems high-speed growth can cause later. The art of good leadership is the ability to look beyond the growth plan and the willingness to act prudently when something is not ready or not right, even if it means slowing things down.

From the 1950s to the '70s, the concept of "forecasting" was considered critical across multiple institutions. Teams of "futurists" were brought in to examine technological, political and cultural trends in order to predict their future impact and prepare for it. (Such a practice may have helped Garmin proactively adapt to advancements in mobile phone technology instead of being forced to react to it.) Even the United States federal government was in on it. In 1972, Congress established the Office of Technology Assessment specifically to examine the long-term impact of proposed legislation. "They're beginning to realize that legislation will remain on the books for 20 or 50 years before it's reviewed," said Edward Cornish, president of the World Future Society, "and they want to be sure that what they do now won't have an adverse impact years from today." However, the discipline fell out of favor during the 1980s, with some in government thinking it a waste of money to try to "predict the future." The office was officially closed in 1995. Though today futurists still exist in the business world, they are usually tasked with helping a company predict trends that can be marketed to rather than assessing future impact of current choices.

Finite-focused leaders are often loath to sacrifice near-term gains, even if it's the right thing to do for the future, because near-term gains are the ones that are most visible to the market. And the pressure this mindset exerts on others in the company to focus on the near-term often comes at the detriment of the quality of the services or the products we buy. That is the exact opposite of what Adam Smith was talking about. If the investor community followed Smith's philosophies, they would be doing whatever they could to help the companies in which they invested make the best possible product, offer the best possible service and build the strongest possible company. It's what's good for the customer and the wealth of nations. And if shareholders really were the owners of the companies in which they invested, that is indeed how they would act. But in reality, they don't act like owners at all. They act more like renters.

Consider how differently we drive a car we own versus one we rent, and all of a sudden it will become clear why shareholders seem more focused on getting to where they want to go with little regard to the vehicle that's taking them there. Turn on CNBC on any given day and we see discussions dominated by talk of trading strategies and near-term market moves. These are shows about trading, not about owning. They are giving people advice on how to buy and flip a house, not how to find a home to raise a family. If short-term-focused investors treat the companies in which they invest like rental cars, i.e., not theirs, then why must the leaders of the companies treat those investors like owners? The fact is, public companies are different from private companies and do not need to conform to the same traditional definition of ownership. If our goal is to build companies that can keep playing for lifetimes to come, then we must stop automatically thinking of shareholders as owners, and executives must stop thinking that they work solely for them. A healthier way for all shareholders to view themselves is as contributors, be they near-term or long-term focused.

Whereas employees contribute time and energy, investors contribute capital (money). Both forms of contribution are valuable and necessary to help a company succeed, so both parties should be fairly rewarded for their contributions. Logically, for a company to get bigger, stronger or better at what they do, executives must ensure that the benefit provided by investors' money or employees' hard work should, as Adam Smith pointed out, go first to those who buy from the company. When that happens, it is easier for the company to sell more, charge more, build a more loyal customer base and make more money for the company and its investors alike. Or am I missing something here? In addition, executives need to go back to seeing themselves as stewards of great institutions that exist to serve all the stakeholders. The impact of which serves the wants, needs and desires of all those involved in a company's success, not just a few.

The fact is, we all want to feel like our work and our lives have meaning. It's part of what it means to be human. We all want to feel a part of something bigger than ourselves. I have to believe this contributes to the reason so many companies say they primarily serve their people and their customers when they are in fact primarily serving their executive ranks and their shareholders. For many of us, even if we don't have the words, the modern form of capitalism we have just feels like something doesn't align with our values. Indeed, if we all truly embraced Friedman's definition of business, then companies would have visions and missions that were solely about maximizing profit and we'd all be fine with it. But they don't. If the true purpose of business was only to make money, there would be no need for so many companies to pretend to be cause or purpose driven. Saying a business exists for something bigger and actually building a business to do it are not the same thing. And only one of those strategies has any value in the Infinite Game.

The Drums of Change Are Beating

In 2018, Larry Fink, the founder, chairman and CEO of BlackRock, Inc., caused a bit of a stir in the financial industry when he wrote an open letter to CEOs titled "A Sense of Purpose." In the letter he urged leaders to build their companies with more idealistic goals than near-term financial gains. "Without a sense of purpose," he explained, "no company, either public or private, can achieve its full potential. It will ultimately lose the license to operate from key stakeholders. It will succumb to short-term pressures to distribute earnings, and, in the process, sacrifice investments in employee development, innovation, and capital expenditures that are necessary for long-term growth." BlackRock, incidentally, is the largest money management firm in the world, with over $6 trillion under management. Though the call for companies to embrace a sense of purpose is not new, when someone of Larry Fink's position in the financial world embraces the concept so publicly, it moves the conversation from articles, books and water coolers to inside palace walls.

The stock market works at its best when it works as it was intended, to allow for the average person to share in the wealth of the nation. However, Americans have become disillusioned with the form of capitalism to which they are subjected today and the way the stock market is used as a tool in a finite game. The share of Americans invested in the stock market is at its lowest point in 20 years. The largest exodus has come from the middle class. People don't mind if an enterprising few make a lot of money. Their exodus is a reaction to the imbalance and a lack of trust in the system . . . and leaders should take notice.

The irony is that everyone who works with or for the public markets understands that when the system becomes too unbalanced, there will always be a correction. That correction is often sudden and violent. Our current system of capitalism is so unbalanced, and those on the inside are well advised to make the necessary corrections themselves, for a failure to do so increases the chances of correction being forced upon them. For if the palace refuses to change from within, it increases the chances that the people will try to knock the whole thing down. Be they against government incompetence, corruption or lopsided economic models, this is what populist uprisings are so often about. Remember the American Revolution itself would have been avoided if Great Britain simply relaxed the economic restrictions it placed on the colonies, gave them greater representation in government and allowed them to share in more of the wealth they helped produce. That's it. Where there is unbalance, there is unrest.

It's a big deal to disrupt a system. Revolutions are fraught with risk. They are sudden. They are violent. And there is almost always a counterrevolution (and when I talk about revolution, I am not only referring to armed insurgencies, I include all kinds of upending to the status quo). The American colonists chose to revolt only after years of appealing for change. Begging for it. They were only partially drawn to revolution for ideological reasons. They were pushed to it because they saw their lives and their economic well-being suffering or restricted as a result of a gross imbalance of power and wealth. The vision of an alternative future came later.

Whether it was in ancient Rome, where the leaders refused to offer citizenship to the allies who suffered to defend Rome, or the American colonists who were refused representation even though their hard work helped fuel the British economy, it is upon the backs of ordinary people that wealth and power are produced. In our modern day and age, it is the employee who bears the most cost for the money companies and their leaders make. They are the ones who must worry every time the company misses its arbitrary projections whether they will be sent home without the means to provide for themselves or their families. It is the employee who comes to work and feels that the company and its leaders do not care about them as human beings (note: offering free food and fancy offices is not the thing that makes people feel cared for). People want to be treated fairly and share in the wealth they helped produce in payment for the cost they bear to grow their companies. I am not demanding it—they are!

The data shows that the current system benefits the top 1 percent of the population disproportionately more than anyone else. In response to that imbalance, a small group of protesters set up camp in Zuccotti Park in New York City in September 2011. They posted signs that said simply, "We are the 99 percent." Leaderless and unfocused, the occupation of parks around the world fizzled but the movement lives on. The spotlight on the fact that the system was rigged for the few at the expense of the masses has not dimmed. If anything, it has grown brighter. Five years since the start of the Occupy movement we heard the populist message rise to the level of a presidential election from Bernie Sanders on the left and Donald Trump on the right. Both candidates fanned the flames about inequality and unfairness of "the system."

The call to abandon Milton Friedman's style of business, like any challenge to any status quo, can come from the people or from the leaders. From outside or from inside. Take heed of the red flags all around us. The rise of a populist voice in America and around the world is growing. And all those in a seat of power—be they in business or in politics—are in a position to effect change. But make no mistake, change is coming. Because that's how the Infinite Game works. This finite system we have now will run itself dry of will and resources eventually. It always does. It always does. Though some may enrich themselves with money or power for now, the system cannot survive under its own weight. If history and almost every stock market crash is any indicator, imbalance is a bitch.

The winds of change are blowing. It has become more socially acceptable to question some of the accepted tenets of Friedman's capitalism. And there continues to be a growing discomfort with such devotion to his definition of the responsibility of business. Organizations like Conscious Capitalism, B Corp, the B Team and others are actively promoting ideas like the stakeholder model or triple bottom line, to challenge Friedman's ideas. And the business heroes of the high flying 1980s and '90s, like Jack Welch, are losing their luster and appeal. It is now self-evident that we need a new definition of the responsibility of business that better aligns with the idea that business is an infinite game. A definition that understands that money is a result and not a purpose. A definition that gives employees and the people who lead them the feeling that their work has value beyond the money they make for themselves, their companies or their shareholders.

Friedman proposed that a business has a single responsibility—profit; a very finite-minded view of business. We need to replace Friedman's definition with one that goes beyond profit and considers the dynamism and additional facets that make business work. In order to increase the infinite value to our nation, our economy and all the companies that play in the game, the definition of the responsibility of business must:

1. Advance a purpose: Offer people a sense of belonging and a feeling that their lives and their work have value beyond the physical work.

2. Protect people: Operate our companies in a way that protects the people who work for us, the people who buy from us and the environments in which we live and work.

3. Generate profit: Money is fuel for a business to remain viable so that it may continue to advance the first two priorities.

Simply put:

The responsibility of business is to use its will and resources to advance a cause greater than itself, protect the people and places in which it operates and generate more resources so that it can continue doing all those things for as long as possible. An organization can do whatever it likes to build its business so long as it is responsible for the consequences of its actions.

The three pillars—to advance a purpose, protect people and generate a profit—seem to be essential in the Infinite

Game. America's founders inspired a nation to come together to advance Life, Liberty and the pursuit of Happiness. These unalienable rights of physical safety, a cause or ideology to be a part of and the opportunity to provide for ourselves inspired a nation and set the United States on its infinite journey. Nearly 150 years later, on December 30, 1922, the Declaration of the Formation of the Soviet Union was ratified. It stated that the new nation of the USSR was founded on the three promises or rights: "All these circumstances imperatively demand the unification of the Soviet republics into one union state, capable of ensuring both external security and internal economic prosperity, and the freedom of the national development of peoples." In other words, a nation committed to protect its people, offer an opportunity of economic gain and advance the ideology of communism. A similar trifecta showed up again during the Vietnam War when General Giap rallied the North Vietnamese to join the People's War with the promise of physical safety, economic advancement and the opportunity to advance an ideology. A People's War is "simultaneously military, economic and political," said Giap in an interview years after the war.

A nation state must protect its citizens, to ensure that we live free from fear. To do that, it must maintain armed forces to defend against foreign threats, establish justice and insure domestic tranquillity. Likewise, inside an organization, a company must provide for the protection of its people by building a culture in which employees feel psychologically safe and feel like their employer cares about them as human beings. We want to know that the company is invested in our growth as much as it is its own. No one should have to come to work in fear of the annual round of layoffs simply because the company missed an arbitrary projection. A company can provide for the safety and protection of those outside its walls by considering how the manufacturing of its products and the ingredients they choose impact the communities in which those products are made or sold.

For nations, our sense of belonging and ideologies that we would sacrifice to advance often come in the form of -isms, like capitalism, socialism and so on. In business, they come in the form of a Just Cause. In both the place we choose to live and the place we choose to make a living, we should feel like we are working to advance something bigger than ourselves.

Among nations, profit matters. Economic prosperity is the ability for the nation to remain solvent. To maintain a strong economy that is well resourced to thrive in good times and survive in lean times. For businesses, it is the same. And both in nations and in companies, everyone wants the opportunity to work hard and earn an income so that we may provide for ourselves and our families.

The goals of a nation founded with an infinite mindset are also the people's goals. A nation exists to serve and include ordinary people as it strives forward. This is what makes us feel emotionally connected to our country, why we feel patriotic. Translated into business terms, it means that a company's goals must also align with people's goals, not simply the goals of shareholders. If we want our work to benefit ourselves, our colleagues, our customers, our communities and the world, then it is right for us to work at companies whose values and goals align with our own. And if they don't, we can demand that they do. Anyone who offers their blood, sweat and tears to advance a company's goals is entitled to feel valued for their contributions and share in the fruits of their labor.

Where Friedman believed the results of our hard work should be for the primary benefit of an elite ruling class (the owner), the more infinite-minded leader would ensure that, so long as there are shared goals, all who contribute will benefit across all three pillars. We are all entitled to feel psychologically protected at work, be fairly compensated for our effort and contribute to something bigger than ourselves. These are our unalienable rights. Business, like any infinite pursuit, is a more powerful force when it is empowered for the people, by the people. Disruption is not going away anytime soon, that's not going to change. How leaders respond to it, however, can. Where Friedman's finite definition of the responsibility focuses on maximizing resources, a revised infinite definition also considers the will of the people.

www.ingramcontent.com/pod-product-compliance
Lightning Source LLC
Chambersburg PA
CBHW081314150726
48001CB00022B/3109